MEDITATIONS WITH
THE CHEROKEE

MEDITATIONS WITH
The Cherokee

*Prayers, Songs, and Stories of
Healing and Harmony*

J. T. Garrett, Ed.D.

Bear & Company
Rochester, Vermont

Bear & Company
One Park Street
Rochester, Vermont 05767
www.InnerTraditions.com

Library of Congress Cataloging-in-Publication Data

Garrett, J. T.
    Meditations with the Cherokee : Prayers, songs, and stories of healing
and harmony / J. T. Garrett.
        p. cm.
    ISBN 1-879181-59-2
    1. Cherokee Indians—Religion. I. Title.
E99.C5 G238 2001
299'.7855—dc21

                                                            2001003442

Printed and bound in the United States

10 9 8 7 6 5 4 3 2 1

Text design and layout by Rachel Goldenberg
This book was typeset in Adobe Garamond with Stone Sans as the display typeface

CONTENTS

PREFACE AND
ACKNOWLEDGMENTS

This book focuses on the meditations of life, rather than on representations of the historical ceremonies that were once an integral part of Cherokee life. It is a journey through old teachings that will often be referred to as the Old Wisdom. The Old Wisdom was taught and shared by several Cherokee elders, including my grandfather. It was referred to as Old Wisdom because the elders did not know where it really originated. Another way to express this is as the old way of our ancestors or "the old ways." It is important for the reader to understand that to preserve the sacredness of various ceremonies and occasions, certain details will not be presented in this book. This is not intended to leave anything out, but to preserve something special for the Cherokee way of life. Cherokee cultural teachings and language reserve certain ceremonial elements as sacred for the members and families of the tribe. These are unique because of tribal heritage. As one elder said to me, "Everyone has their own understanding in mind and spirit for those things that are sacred to them. When sacred to someone else it is to be respected and understood as unique for them, not for us to know or understand. Be thankful for whatever is shared, because it is a gift." I thank the many elders who shared with me, so that I can share with you.

I want to thank the Cherokee elders who meant so much to me while I was learning Cherokee Medicine. I will do this with tobacco prayers when the book is published, as they do not wish to be recognized. While respecting their wish as Medicine Men and Medicine Women, I also want to honor their memories; with a couple of exceptions, all of these elders have passed on to the other world. These men and women used their gifts and were helpers to many. Their time and sharing was a very special gift to me. Those elders will stay in my spirit, and their names will stay in my heart. I am glad to share some of their wisdom with you.

The Cherokee elders who taught me Indian Medicine also encouraged me to share with others, but with caution. As one elder said, "Sharing is also opening yourself up to those who would have other intentions. When you write a book or publish an article, it is out there for anyone to see and hear. If they are true of heart, then they will appreciate and respect your words. And that must be your focus. Don't worry about those who differ with your teachings; just recognize and show respect for their way. Keep yourself clear and protected from those who are of another mind. Just let them know this is your way, your teaching and understanding. Wa do (Skee)! (Thank you!)

My vision was always to be a teacher and writer, rather than a healer. When I taught the healing, it was in a group setting. Little did I know back then that I would become a health and hospital administrator in my career, as well as an environmental health professional. In retrospect, this seems fitting to my way of life. My initial interest in biology and botany was satisfied with my enjoyment of herbal remedies and keeping up with the latest advances for good health choices. My vision became my way of life in later years.

I want to thank my mother for encouraging me to use caution, but to continue my vision. My father passed away in May 1978, but he encouraged me to continue my studies in the traditional teachings while completing my formal doctoral degree in public health. Being from a long line of Irish who suffered their own experiences, he wanted me to be educated and free to make my own choices in my life. Near his passing I could see the gleam in his very weak eyes that assured me of my path. Those strengths in my youth started me early on my path to be independent and to make positive life choices.

Several of the Cherokee and other American Indian tribal elders felt that a sign had come in the form of a star or comet, allowing for information to be shared that would otherwise not have been shared. They referred to it as a sign of changing time that, from that celestial moment forward, people would be able to listen to and understand the ways of American Indians for the survival of Mother Earth. The time was 1987. According to one of the elders, "The sign was clear for us to go back to the real reason we are here on Mother Earth, to be a protector of her, as we relearn to be a helper to humans and all living things on Mother Earth." Several elders encouraged me to listen to the signs of Nature. Several events captured my attention, but no one sign or event was a clear message. The passing of Doc Amoneeta Sequoyah in 1981 and his message to listen closely to the changes in Mother Earth made me more aware of the time of change coming about in 1987. Clearly, it was time for many cultures to come together and for more of the Old Wisdom to be shared.

I want to thank my daughter, Melissa, and my son, Michael, for encouraging me to share this gift of information learned from the elder Medicine Men and Women of the Eastern Band of Cherokee Indians. Myrtle Driver has been a very special friend and interpreter of the Cherokee language and the Old Wisdom. Frances Reed has been especially helpful with the pronunciation of Cherokee words and expressions. Many in my tribe have shared with me and encouraged me to write this book and to continue writing and presenting this important information on Cherokee wisdom. I especially want to thank Ella Sequoyah, whose husband was Doc Amoneeta Sequoyah. He was my teacher and mentor for many years in Cherokee. His special gift and Ella's special way of encouragement, her smile and laugh as a way to communicate, helped me to "look beyond the treetops" for special guidance in my life.

Wa do (Skee) to all who have encouraged me to share and preserve the Cherokee teachings for future generations.

INTRODUCTION TO
CHEROKEE WISDOM TEACHINGS

The traditions and early teachings of the Cherokee and other North American Indians provide us with keys to unlock the "Old Wisdom," or old ways. These culturally oriented traditions provide values and knowledge about nature that can help all of us in preserving Mother Earth. We are one with Mother Earth. Destruction of her is destruction of ourselves.

Understanding these lost social and spiritual ways of American Indians is critical to our survival in the future. After all, survival was the primary basis of almost all actions in an earlier time. While our perceptions about survival have changed, our feeling about the need to go on is primarily unchanged in our collective memory, or "spirit memory." It seems ironic to me that survival groups replete with fortresses and guns have formed to protect their members against other people. In an earlier time it was more likely to be other mammals that were considered a threat; they were stronger and faster and would eat us for *their* survival. In a sense, our basic and innate needs for food and health are about the same today as they were in the early beginnings of human and animal life. Our influences, both internal and external, socialize our lives. As a Cherokee elder said to me, "Anyone who thinks they can survive 'alone' will not survive. We are here today [as American Indians] because we are families and tribes."

Everything we do affects all our relations and the survival of our species. We are all connected to our ancestors in spirit and in the physical being within ourselves. The past, present, and future are on the same energy continuum. This spirit memory will form links among the stories and teachings in this book.

In my experience as an apprentice of Cherokee Medicine, I noticed much about survival in the old ways and stories. This book will focus on some of these wonderful stories and teachings of the Old Wisdom.

As a point of reference, I will capitalize the term Medicine when referring to Cherokee or Indian Medicine. Cherokee Medicine is a way of life that includes the physical, mental, spiritual, and natural. Its focus is on the basis of survival, and an understanding that goes beyond practices and words, which do not always connect us with the spirit memory. It is that spirit memory that connects us to our early cultural experience.

Spirit memory is written in our DNA, and in every cell of our body. Cherokee teachings say that we are connected to our ancestors in spirit memory. Our ancestors look over us and are with us always. We can communicate with them at will. As one Cherokee elder put it, "We cannot survive tomorrow without knowing our past. Our ancestors are here with us, but we have to call upon them and be willing to listen. If we don't learn and understand about that, we will not have a future. Their teachings are not about a fortress against our aggressor; they are about love for mankind and all other living creatures on Mother Earth. They are more than lessons to learn; they are learned lessons to understand and to apply to our way of life. As the earlier ancestors did, we must do, or not survive."

This is the story of *Meditations with the Cherokee*. To understand the Cherokee stories one must be willing to accept another way of life, the life of the early Cherokee. The term *survival* means more than being part of a television program of people on a remote island fighting the natural elements. Survival in the Old Wisdom is about understanding yourself and having a deep connection and being in harmony with your natural surroundings. This book will not teach us how to survive, but our survival may depend on what this book has to teach us.

This book is about the Cherokee way of life, but it could just as easily be the ancient teachings of any culture of people here on Mother Earth today. In its simplicity it is a wonderful way of life that has much to teach us all about every culture of people that has survived today. The Cherokee culture, as an elder put it, "is known for not being the best hunters, but for hunting the best." The focus was not on the individual, but on family, clan, and the like.

Meditation in this book becomes more a devotional exercise of contemplation. It is intended with exercises and activities to be dynamic in the process of reflecting and actualizing. Meditation becomes that state of being aware of ourselves in the circle of life.

As a point of reference for the reader, the Cherokee people were taught that they were the Principal People. Rather than an ego-based term, this term reflects the belief that the Cherokee were once part of a larger group that was, over time, somehow split. For purposes of this book the who or why or where of this split do not matter. What is important is that the Cherokee Old Wisdom is thought to have connections with other cultures somewhere in time. Ironically, the Cherokee did not focus on time; not even the language made reference to future. There was just presence, today. The past was in the spirit hands of the ancestors. Some old stories indicated that the Cherokee came from the stars and from a spirit people referred to as the Universal Circle. From the stories passed down through my grandfather and other elders, I learned that we were a mix of many different people, banding together for survival in the wilderness and the harsh environment. From that awareness I learned the true meaning of respecting all others, both animals and humans, as our brothers and sisters. The stories suggest that some of the Cherokee people came from the South. Sequoyah, or George Guess, was a famous Cherokee who wanted to record the Cherokee language. He invented the Cherokee alphabet, which was approved by the Cherokee chiefs in 1821. From the stories Sequoyah heard as a child, he believed that the Cherokee came from the South. Sequoyah spent his final days in travel, searching for those connections.

As a member of the Eastern Band of Cherokee Indians, I find that the stories passed down in my tribe seem more logical than archeological. They constitute the living history of a living people that has somehow survived to tell their story. The stories tell of survival since the beginning of time, or at least since the beginning of the oral history of a tribal people that has survived.

From an American Indian perspective, we are all kin to each other in the Universal Circle of life, including every animal and bird, every living thing on Mother Earth. In other words, we are all connected with some common element in nature. The earlier Cherokee did not need genetic proof or genomes to determine common threads that linked us together. The elder Medicine Men told us of these things many generations ago. They taught that we are dependent on each other, and Mother Earth is dependent on us. As one Cherokee-Natchez elder put it, "We like to think we are independent as individuals and as people of different cultures on Mother Earth. Everything that happens to one of us happens to all of us. The Great One connected us all to elemental life energy itself. If we hurt another, we hurt ourselves. Every young Cherokee learns that everything is our brother and sister. There is a reason why this is taught and why this is true. It comes from the Old Wisdom taught by the Old Ones, who were from another dimension and time. They understood these things, and we must understand them too, to survive each other."

An understanding of the Old Wisdom begins with an appreciation of the beauty of Mother Earth and Nature Herself. The miracle of reproduction teaches us about acceptance. I call this the "Rule of Acceptance"; that rule helps us to appreciate what is, and simply being as a way of life. It is not about striving to change everything for the better. The Rule of Acceptance says that just appreciating something for what it is really worth to us is good enough. As harsh and unforgiving as Nature can be, we can never improve on the creation that is around us every day. Probably the best we can do is clean up our own mess.

Meditation activities and exercises give us a rare opportunity to learn the Rule of Acceptance by simply allowing our connection with Nature and the Universal Circle to open to us. As young Cherokee, one of the first things we learn is to be helpers and protectors of this sacred connection with Mother Earth. We are taught to respect and accept our connection with the animals, birds, and other creatures here on Mother Earth, as well as with other human beings.

It is with honor to my Cherokee elders and respect for the traditional heritage that I am willing to share some of the Old Wisdom. As one elder put it, "You take a chance in sharing with others, because they have their own story. Even those in our own tribe have their own story, so it is good for you to say this is your story. Collectively, it is a story that belongs to all of us, if we could go far enough back to be as one again." Acceptance of life and everything around us is a traditional element of Cherokee thinking. Critical thinking was not a part of what I call the Rule of Acceptance. As you read this book accept what you will, and use this information in a way that is comfortable for you. You have your own beliefs, and neither I, nor any Cherokee teacher would want to take those from you. It is difficult for me to imagine any group imposing its will on a gentle and family-oriented people such as the Cherokee were in an earlier time. However, possession of land and expansion changed forever the lives of the Cherokee. It is my desire that anyone reading this book will be changed in a positive way because they want that change. To Cherokee of that earlier time, choice, humility, and respect for everything was paramount. All was for the benefit of the tribe and the family over any advantage for the individual.

The Old Wisdom also teaches us that we have a connection to a greater and more powerful energy, regardless of what we choose to call it. Earlier Cherokee expressions of that energy would be

"Yo wa," or "E to da" as our father above, and "E tsi i" as our mother below. To understand and accept this connection is to realize that we can communicate with this special energy in our own way. Relearning to communicate with nature will connect us to a beautiful reality. The wonder of that magical connection is its openness and acceptance. That connection also opens the door to the past and the future, which are present with us now. The activities and exercises in this book will allow for this reconnection with Nature.

While reconnecting is simple, it takes a shift in mindset to be comfortable with Nature as a connection to the Universal Circle. The activities in this book are focused on putting us back in touch with Nature and our spirit self again. As we open up to our natural sense of connection, the stories and meditations put us in touch with a natural intelligence and way of communicating that brings us messages. As my grandfather and other Cherokee elders taught me, to accept this awareness is to open the doors of time into the past and the future. This book will open doors for a profound understanding of life, allowing you an opportunity to change your feelings and so influence your thinking toward a calmer you, bringing resolve about your purpose and commitment to family and yourself and other creations here on Mother Earth.

In this book I will refer to American Indians and Alaska Natives as Native Americans. However, most persons who are a member of a specific American Indian tribe or band would prefer to be identified by their specific tribal name. The official name for various American Indians in the United States is their tribal name, such as Eastern Band of Cherokee or Cherokee Nation, rather than just Cherokee.

I studied with many tribal elders, whom I refer to in this book as elders. That alone is considered a very respected title among American Indians. However, Beloved Elder is a title given to some because of very special life deeds for the tribe. I want to honor their memory and show respect for their sharing of traditional knowledge and teachings by sharing a "Tsa lu," or tobacco prayer.

Share a pinch of pipe-smoking tobacco with Mother Earth, while you give thanks to the Great One for whatever it is you are thankful for today. A tobacco prayer I like to use is as follows.

"Oh, Gi daw da (Oh, Great One), I offer this sacred tobacco, Tsa lu. I am thankful for E tsa e, E lo he no (Mother Earth). I am thankful for A tse lah (Fire) of life. Gift me with healing and the ability to be a helper to others, as you would have me be a helper to others. Wa do (Skee) (Thank you).

In each of the meditation chapters are messages directed to you, the individual reader. Do keep in mind, though, that the teachings in the Old Wisdom are not about us pondering the questions of truth just about ourselves. The teachings are about our relationships. Look and listen to the spirit message that seems to relate most closely to you. This is particularly true when animal and stone spirits are mentioned. Once you are connected to Mother Earth with the spirit animal and stone, then it is right to allow yourself to think and feel more openly about your relationships with all things.

This book will take you on a journey of discovery about relationships. You will find some truths that will connect you to an old memory that lies deep within your subconscious. Your many other senses will come into play, which will provide a greater sense of connection and guidance.

For the Cherokee, past and present, meditation in its many forms is a way of life. I encourage you to integrate the activities and exercises in this book, these "ways," into your life, your journey, your way.

1

IN THE BEGINNING

Early Cherokee myths and stories told of the beginning of life. Everything was equal and all was kin to one another. There was no dominant group or society. Equality meant that the small earthworm was just as important as the chief of the bears. Every animal, bird, and creature had its own gifts and purpose in life. Even when the humans came into being, their gift of reason and will did not make them any more dominant than any other animal. In fact, every human spirit was connected to an animal, bird, or plant. That was the only way humans came into physical being here on Mother Earth. Every human's purpose was to be a helper to all the rest of creation in the Universal Circle.

Survival in life was based on being a helper and protector of all life in the Universal Circle while also being helped and receiving protection. In the beginning the humans were taught that for every action there was a consequence affecting all other life. No action, not even a thought, would go without some consequence or reaction within the Universal Circle. Respect for life was so important that one would starve rather than taking another life without permission, without asking the spirit of the animal for food, and fur for warmth.

One life was not dominant over another life here on Mother Earth. We as humans were connected in spirit to all the animals, birds, and creations on Mother Earth. This connection is still emphasized in the Cherokee teachings today. The other creatures are part of our ancestry, and guide us as mentors while we are in physical life.

In a sense, the Cherokee do not distinguish past, present, and future tenses. All existence since the beginning is here with us now. The ancestors are living beings in spirit that are here to teach us in this life, and include plants, trees, and even rocks, such as crystals, which were created with life energy.

The Cherokee have always believed in one supreme energy being. This Great One, or Great Spirit, is somewhere in the sky vault above us. This universal spirit, "Oh Gi daw da," in the everyday language or "Yo wa" in the old language certainly had a hand in our creation. There is often reference to a Great Council whose members created us as beings of energy with special abilities and gifts. We are part of this larger spirit within the Universal Circle. Our life depends on the Universal Circle, and everything we do affects that circle.

The stories shared by our Cherokee elders are the primary source for our understanding of the beginning of time, and the lessons that all of us must learn about life. Of course, much in the teachings has been influenced by other religions that came to these shores. Ironically, the Cherokee were able to keep their traditional beliefs from the old teachings alongside their new religions. The same cannot be said about several of the religious groups regarding Native American beliefs. This is a subject that I prefer not to discuss any further. Individuals all have their own beliefs about the advantages and disadvantages of religious influence. Fortunately, even with the influence from others, many of the Cherokee stories and myths remained intact.

Since this is a book of meditations, our thought process will focus on the positive, what the elders would call "Good Medicine" teachings and influence.

American Indians refer to North America as Turtle Island. The stories told by American Indians of others who came to Turtle Island are usually negative because of the disease and destruction that resulted. The ideas of expansion and possession of land were not in the daily reality of American Indians. However, there are some quite positive writings from observations made by travelers with the purpose of recording the Native American way of life. This is all we have in writing of the earlier sacred ceremonies and rituals of the Cherokee at that time. I want to mention them as a reference for readers interested in greater detail. A source I have always admired is an article by John Howard Payne in the *Quarterly Register and Magazine* from December of 1849 (pages 444–450). Titled "The Ancient Cherokee Traditions and Religious Rites," this very good source provides real-life experience of the rituals and traditions of the Cherokee. There were others, such as Henry Timberlake, James Adair, William Bartram, and James Mooney, who also recorded useful information. Mooney documented original Cherokee manuscripts, archeology, religion, songs, ceremonies, and much more about the sacred formulas of the Cherokee. His papers were written from extensive notes that he gathered while living among the Cherokee from 1887 to 1890. These papers were published in the Seventh Annual Report of the Bureau of American Ethnology in 1891, with an extensive listing of herbal uses. I became familiar with these writings while working with the Cherokee Historical Association.

The travelers to Cherokee country during those years provided observations and secondhand information to the reader. Sometimes Cherokee informants would say what they thought the travelers wanted to hear. Language barriers played a role in interpretation of information. Observations could be in error, particularly with reference to plants, and even to ceremonies. However, these writings do provide a snapshot of Cherokee rituals and ways by someone visiting with the Cherokee at that time.

As this book is interested more in the living information for meditations than on archeological or historical records, I take my information on the meanings of various ceremonies from accounts by elders. My apprenticeship in Cherokee Indian Medicine, with some thirty-five years as a student and teacher, will suffice, without reference to the sources mentioned above.

Cherokee Medicine Men (and Women)

From a very early age I felt a wonderful sense of "the way it used to be" from listening to the Cherokee elders tell stories. My time with my teacher, Doc Amoneeta Sequoyah, was very special. I can still hear him sing his chant with his beaded turtle rattle. Listening to the elders made it easy for me to imagine a time when the Cherokee roamed many miles, covering an area the size of several states.

Special terms were used to describe Cherokee Medicine and traditions. The elders would talk about the "way." This usually referred to the old way or traditional way of doing things, or a ceremony. Another expression, "as it was told to me," described the stories passed down through many generations of Cherokee. Sometimes the elders would even speak things in Cherokee, in the "old language" or "the old way of telling it," as they would say. Because my grandfather had passed away when I was very young, I adopted Doc Amoneeta as my grandfather to teach me about Cherokee Medicine. He was a wonderful elder with a keen sense of humor. Working with him was a great pleasure because he helped me to keep everything in perspective. I had other teachers, both male and female, who prefer to not be named. They have long since passed on to the other world, as has Doc Sequoyah.

My spoken Cherokee leaves a lot to be desired. As it was not my first language, interpretation was sometimes confusing to me. Some words in Cherokee are used only in certain ceremonies, at certain times, by those trained to speak or chant the "old" words. Some of these words were so sacred that to speak of them in common terms could cost you your life—at least that was what I was told.

I would listen intently for hours as the elders shared stories with me. Many times an elder would come up to me and say, "I bet you haven't heard this one," and then start telling me a story. Most of the stories were spoken as though the storyteller had been there when the event happened, or as though the event were going on even as we talked. There was no past or present tense, just a moving picture before us as the story was being told.

Fortunately, Myrtle Driver from Big Cove was my special friend and an official interpreter for the tribe. She knew much about the old stories and the old language of the early Cherokee. Many times I called her about certain words. Being a thoughtful and patient person, she would reply, "Why don't you just say it in English?" Cherokee is a beautiful language to hear and to speak, but unless you speak the language on a daily basis, it is difficult to get the right flow and inflections. I have felt extremely honored to have learned from the earlier visitors to the Smoky Mountains and to have heard the stories and sharing of information by the elders in my lifetime.

The title of this chapter is "In the Beginning." To start, or begin-again, we must reaffirm our humility as a helper to all other humans and animals, to the winged ones and all creatures, plants, and trees, as they are helpers to us. In the Cherokee way of life we recognize the Great One and all his powers of creation, such as Sun and Moon, the thunder beings that bring us rain and cleansing, and the power of life. We recognize the power of the Four Directions of physical, mental, spiritual, and natural gifts in our circle of life and the Universal Circle. We offer tobacco in our own way, and we pray. We celebrate life and enjoy being a protector of Mother Earth and a helper to all others. We respect and honor our elders and teach the children the way of right relationship. We give thanks each day and live life to honor our family, clan, and tribe. Wa do (Skee)!

To start in the beginning we have to start with a meditation on the sweat lodge ceremony, or "Asi." This ceremony is a traditional way to prepare oneself to speak with or get messages from the ancestors. In our busy lives it is often difficult to take time for traditional sweats, and many people are not trained for such ceremonies. Other ways of meditation can be used for preparing the body and heart to receive messages from the spirit world.

This first exercise will be our way of going back to the beginning.

Sweat Lodge Ceremony

In this meditation we will focus on using our imagination to draw on a spirit memory of another time. In the old Cherokee stories there is almost always a reference to the beginning of time, or "in the beginning." Always, "in the beginning" there was darkness; the original idea of a sweat lodge was providing a way for a person to go back to the feeling of that beginning time, that moment before creation.

Settle yourself in a totally dark place, either in a closed room or outside in a protected area, preferably at the time of the full moon or new moon. Light a purple candle; play some comfortable Native American flute or soft drumming music to set the mood. If you don't start with music or a chant of some kind, you will have difficulty turning off your thoughts. Have a pad and paper or a small recorder handy to record events that you want to remember, preferably after the experience. Do not worry about recording everything or missing something. Your mind and spirit will help you remember, or help you "clear" something that you do not want to remember.

If you feel cool, wrap up in a blanket. Once you are settled, begin the meditation.

 Imagine yourself entering a sweat lodge. The purpose of going into an earth-covered cave or lodge is to return to the beginning of the birth time. You are comfortable and protected with a covering surrounding you. Sit cross-legged, or get into another comfortable position. You can use comfortable pillows, or even rest your back against something firm. You want to move into a different mind state from a totally relaxed sense. You want to achieve a keen level of awareness and sensitivity while you let all your intensity and stress go.

You are in your sacred space. Totally shut out your thought processing and let your mind just relax. Call upon Grandmother Spirit and your spirit guide to protect you and to be with you during the entire "sweat" process.

Stare at the candle and allow your eyes to feel relaxed enough to close on their own. As your eyes begin to close, focus on going back to your own beginning. Keep aware of the space around you, knowing that you are safe and protected. You have total control, and can "come up" or awaken any time you please. Enjoy the experience as you relax, possibly totally relax, for the first time in your own sacred sweat lodge. This is not about the reality of the location, but about the reality of your own experience. This is your time to receive messages or to have your own vision.

Allow yourself to create your own story. Many old stories were created by watching the animals, then asking the animal spirits to come forward as a story was created. Does one animal spirit come very strongly to you? This is probably your animal spirit.

An elder once told me that if we imagine the sweat lodge the experience is real, because we carry the ancient memory of this experience. You are connecting with memory and communicating with your own spirit guides. The key is to receive, not to relive past experiences. The story you allow to come to you will always has some special value that you can use in your personal life or share with others. This is your vision.

With practice, you can imagine a sweat lodge and have your own vision experience quite quickly. This is to be an enjoyable experience. If you have any difficulty at all in the experience, just stop. It may be necessary to consult someone who understands the Sweat Lodge Ceremony in order to evoke a positive and vision-seeking experience.

The sweat lodge meditation can become a recurrent ceremony that will create understanding for harmony and balance. It can also be a helper to make you more aware and sensitive to the living world around you.

In earlier years, the more sensitive a person was to his or her gift of senses the better that person could hunt and survive in a wild and hostile environment. In a way, it is not much different for us today. An elder once said to me, "Everything that ever was is still with us and a part of us. We are the continuing circle of life, and every circle that ever was has merged into our circle. We still hunt and gather. We reproduce, live, get ill, heal, and eventually pass on to the other world."

Medicine Bag

In earlier times certain helpmates were gathered and kept close at hand to keep strong one's connection to the Universal Circle. An Indian would not be without a personal Medicine bag. That bag would contain items connecting the owner to past ancestors and protecting him or her from present influences.

The next exercise is for you to create your own Medicine Bag. If you have one, consider other things that can go into your bag or bundle for your own Medicine.

There is so much in Indian Medicine that is difficult to describe using words. In an earlier time we focused more on feelings and less on words when providing instruction. At the risk of oversimplifying Indian Medicine, in this exercise imagine the special box you had as a child where you kept the things that were important to you. To American Indians, a Medicine bundle or Medicine bag includes all things that influence or affect one's life. The bundle may include a piece of tobacco that goes back four generations, or an arrowhead that came from family ancestry and connects that person with her past. The bundle might include a prayer or a song that was shared at special occasions or ceremonies. The contents of one's bag are all sacred, and a part of the past, present, and future.

This short description is meant to assist you in understanding how important it is to realize our connection with Nature. Mother Earth is a part of our Medicine. When we become disconnected from her, we lose a part of ourselves that is our true inheritance as an energy being called human. Therefore, our first journey in understanding ourselves is to reconnect to the beginning.

What should you have in your Medicine bag? I will describe what is in mine, to give you some ideas. I have several Medicine bags. One bag carries the herbs that are part of my Medicine. There are seven of them, including Yellow Root, which is used for sore throats. Since I speak a lot to groups, this is important to have for my tea. I have another bundle just for my sacred tobacco, particularly since the smell of tobacco can affect everything else. I keep the tobacco in this separate bag, along with some sage that was gifted to me by a Sioux Medicine Man. The tobacco, *Nicotiana rustica,* is commonly referred to as ancient tobacco, or "Tsa lu." Instead of wild tobacco, regular smoking tobacco is fine for sharing with Mother Earth, with the fire, and with friends who need a tobacco prayer. Keep in mind that I do not smoke this tobacco. It is solely for ceremonial and prayer purposes.

Another Medicine bundle, a small deerskin bag that hangs from my neck, includes a special crystal with a small pinch of sacred tobacco. The crystal is one cleared by my daughter, Melissa, who has been trained in the Crystal Medicine. This special gift of a small crystal is for protection.

A large Medicine bag contains all the little gifts given to me over the years. These items include special rocks, gemstones, a small piece of wood from a tree struck by lightning, silver pieces, crystals, feathers, herbs, pieces of pottery from very old Indian sites, ashes, gifts from my grandmother and grandfather, arrowheads, a knife from my father, and sundry other special or sacred items.

It is important to not allow others to go through your Medicine bag and touch your special items. Remember, each of those items has its own special energy. It is very important that you do not let others touch your crystals. Crystals are like little batteries that store their own energy. Touching them—especially touching the tip or energy apex—can interfere with the energy of the crystal. The Medicine bundle contains all in our lives that we have learned to guide us.

Origin Stories

In earlier years, stories told by the elders were based on wisdom that provided values. These values were to guide the morals and even the business of the family, clan, or tribe. They connected us with our ancestors, and they too became part of our Medicine bundles.

The Cherokee elders would say that every story has a familiar memory to us. These memories are recorded in every cell of our bodies going back to the beginning, whenever that may have been. Sometimes Native Americans will refer to that beginning as the time when our ancestors and every connection we have ever had in our existence as a tribal people were here.

While there may be many stories on the origin of the creation, there is one story about the birth of our ancestors and our connection to all other living things here on Mother Earth.

In the beginning of time, Mother Earth was a celestial body floating in the universe, like a great island floating in a sea of water. The island, suspended by invisible cords at four points, or directions, in the sky vault, was a solid rock formation that had special energy like a magnet. The old ones told of the cords being delicate, and they feared that one day those cords would break. Then the island would sink into the ocean of the universe and become the flow of water energy for all time.

All spirits were in the sky vault in a place called ga Lun La di ehi.

During one of the councils with the Great One, the animal spirits asked for more room, since it was getting crowded in ga Lun La di ehi, or their father's place. Water Beetle was the first to go see what was below. Because she was Beaver's grandchild, the animal spirits thought she would be able to fly and land on a surface in the water. She flew and flew but found no place to land. Finally, she dove into the water to discover there was mud, which clung to her as she moved back to the surface. The animals were so excited that they provided what we know as gut string to tie the dried mud in the four directions to provide balance to Mother Earth.

Great Buzzard, one of the Bird tribe, was sent to find a place suitable for each of the tribes to locate. When he flew over the area he found that the mud was still very soft. Being tired, he let one of his wings dip into the mud, which created valleys and mountains. Today, we know that area as Cherokee country, because of the beautiful Smoky Mountains and the Blue Ridge Mountains. There are still places in the valley called Buzzard's Place.

It was time for the four-legged ones, the winged ones, and all of the Great One's creations to come down to this new place in the sky vault. As one elder told me, the Great One sent the Thunder Beings to give a special life energy to Mother Earth. He also asked Sun to be the father over this new land, knowing that the Great One was very busy with everything in the Universal Circle. Also, the land was dark until Nu Dah, or the Sun, and Grandmother Moon watched by day and night. While this was the beginning for Mother Earth, the early Cherokee knew that there were other worlds out there in the Universal Circle with "apportioners," such as the Sun, the Moon, and Thunder Beings, who oversee those worlds.

All living things on Mother Earth were to be brothers and sisters to one another. As there was opposite energy, so would there be balance and equality for all. The sacred teachings, or old wisdom, of the Cherokee and all tribes would protect that balance, so that all creatures on Mother Earth and in the Universal Circle could live in harmony.

And so it was that all the animals and creatures, big and small, would live in peace on Mother Earth.

While there are many stories of the origin of our creation, the Cherokee stories focus on equality and sacredness of all living things here on Mother Earth. This lesson reminds us that everything on Mother Earth is our brother and sister.

It is said that we humans can revisit or reconnect to the beginning, that we possess the unusual ability to revisit a place in time, going back to the beginning of another era of life. In the next meditation, read each sentence in the paragraph one at a time, closing your eyes after each sentence and allowing your mind to take you on the journey. I was always told to go out into Nature if my imagination could not take me on a journey through a past time. Sitting in Nature helps to ease the mind and enables us to tap into the special flow of energy that we refer to as images or pictures. The early Cherokee referred to these pictures as messages from our ancestors, who are here to guide us.

This meditation will connect you with universal energy and memory, with your own experience of the human origin story.

The purpose is to open your energy to the sense of warm connection with the Sun. Once you can feel this sense of warmth, you can do the same meditation to feel your connection with others: animals, humans, plants, and all our relations. This meditation takes us back to the basic connection of our energy with the beginning of life.

The Sun is bright, but a cloudy haze shelters you from the direct rays while you still feel the Sun's warmth. The Sun is Nu Dah, the first element made by the Great One, or Universal Spirit. Close your eyes and feel the warmth of Nu Dah as you journey back to the beginning of time. Understand that the element of Sun was made first. Feel the calm and peace of the first warmth, and the love from its gift of warmth. Eyes closed, experience this warmth and love for a few minutes.

We are born from the fire in the womb and the spark of life in the universal sky vault, sometimes referred to as heaven. In this meditation we will go from the openness of outside connection to the Sun to the warmth and comfort of being nurtured and supported by Mother Earth. Imagine that you are being born from a place of darkness—put your hands over your eyes for a few seconds, then gradually move them outward and open them up to the light in front of you while you keep your eyes closed. Feel the warmth and comfort of light that the Sun provides you in life. Experience this opening and sense of comfort with no strain or stress as you slowly open your eyes. The movement is slow, with a sense of natural calm.

We are introduced to Grandmother Moon as the Sun goes down slowly in the horizon. In darkness we are always protected by the Moon. Imagine yourself standing and looking at the Moon, or go outside in the evening. Reaching out to Grandmother Moon with our hands closed together, we feel her presence. Like the Sun, she is also known as Nu Dah. Grandmother Moon knows us; she is a part of us. In the evening's coolness she wraps us in her warmth like a blanket, looking over us while we rest our physical bodies. She is our keeper in the physical world and in the spirit world. The fire we build at night, in the wood stove and in our bodies, keeps us warm and protected as we feel the love of Grandmother Moon. She is always there, even when the Sun comes up again on the horizon.

Experience Grandmother Moon with you as the Sun goes down in the horizon, until you are ready for the Sun to peek out from the distant horizon, in the early morning of your life.

A Universal Circle surrounds us while Nu Dah protects our balance in life. The cycles of the Sun and Moon guide our mood and spirit. In a sense this circle, or spirit, has boundaries, and in another sense it is without boundary. Within this circle of life we choose our own harmony. This is where we are given guidance in spirit. In the silence of your room, or in nature, ask for spirit guidance. Then listen with your heart and mind. What do you hear?

Each of us is unique and different, yet alike in our ability to experience this thing we call life. In the beginning we could communicate with animals and with all things created in this Universal Circle. We had no limitations, not even in time. With your eyes closed or open, experience the freedom that we had as shapeless energies, able to float in this open space, yet somehow connected to something that we cannot yet explain. For a few moments, simply let all pain go as you move effortlessly with calm and comfort in this space.

The place we call Mother Earth becomes our home as we come from the spirit world into the physical world. Now we are ready to feel our connection and relation to Mother Earth. She grounds our physical body as well as our spirit. Touch Mother Earth with your hands, or lay on her in a comfortable position. What do you feel?

Given a will and the need to survive, we are dependent on all things here on Mother Earth. As one elder put it, "We think we are independent and that all our actions are without reactions, unless we will it to be that way. In fact, we are connected to every action, with reactions or consequences for everyone else that we are connected to in this physical world." While Nu Dah was apportioned the responsibility to maintain balance in our lives, everything else is our choice and will. We are the keepers of all things and the protectors of Mother Earth. That simple reality pervades every part of our being and is integrated into every religion and lesson in life.

Stop reading at this time and go visit a plant or flower. For a few minutes, just be open to the sense of uniqueness of the plant or flower. Then see the reflection of your own uniqueness in that plant or flower. How are you alike and how are you different from each other? Everything on Mother Earth has a purpose and survives for that purpose. Observe the texture and shape of the leaves and the flowers. They were the first spirits on Mother Earth that made it possible for us to take a breath, as they inhaled carbon dioxide and exhaled oxygen. Now we can breathe! Take a few deep breaths and slowly exhale as you give thanks for these gifts of Nature. We are to protect them, as we do our four-legged friends and the winged ones. It is the Indian way, and the way of life for every living two-legged one. As humans we are truly the "humus" of life. Spend some time just walking around in Nature to experience the feelings and sensations of being among the plants that surround you. A Cherokee elder said, "The plants were here before us. They gave us our first breath. They provide food and medicine for us to survive. Even when the animals met in council in the beginning years to give us diseases, the plants defended us. While the animals were being abused by the humans, the plants said they would provide medicine and healing for us. They are a gift to us with each breath of life. Wa do (Skee)!"

Ceremony and expressions of joy in giving thanks have always been a core expression of the American Indian way of life. Now it is time to celebrate and enjoy life as a circle of energy. Move around the room, or in the outdoor area in which you've been meditating. Let your body move and flow at will. How does it feel?

Ceremony is an expression of song, dance, sharing of food, and sharing of stories to keep the traditions alive in the hearts and minds of young people. The adults and elders share the stories and song-chants that their ancestors passed down to them. Somewhere in time there was a sound or grunt that took on a sense of rhythm. Make a sound and allow it to lead you into an audible chant. Breathe deeply as you chant. How does it feel?

Ceremony is about giving thanks. Find your own way to simply give thanks to the Great One for life by saying in your own words, "Thank you, Great One, for this day. I will listen to my guides and honor this day with everything I do and say."

Connecting with Nature

To revisit our beginning in meditation, we must first reorient ourselves to Nature and the natural wisdom that exists beyond the limited mental thinking in our daily lives. Reconnecting with Mother Earth is a form of traditional "clearing-way" that helps us feel good inside. One does not have to go to the outside environment to reconnect; you can simply get plants together and sit as close to them as possible while you meditate. The energy of the plants helps guide the meditation to a simpler level, from which you can receive messages on anything from life to love. Connecting with Nature, your thoughts become pure and innocent once again. Words such as respect, honor, and pride seem to come out in those messages with the clear life energy of plants, flowers, and trees.

Breathe deeply and slowly while you focus on clearing the cobwebs in your mind and spirit. This guided activity may help.

Sit outside under a tree, or inside with plants surrounding you. The key is to be in a place where you feel protected while you meditate. Take three deep breaths and close your eyes, or else gently focus your vision on something relaxing, such as a flower. When ready, close your eyes and notice your breathing.

While relaxing, thank the Great One for this wonderful day. Ask for guidance as you open your mind and spirit for messages from Nature. She always has some simple messages to share.

While being guided, every few seconds say the word *love* to allow yourself the open feeling of clear connection with the natural spirit of the environment. This is one of the few words that allows for the image of giving and receiving at the same time.

Refocus, with eyes open or closed, on the flower or other element that you focused on in initiating the meditation. Relax and enjoy the images and messages that come to you. Your natural senses will eventually connect with the energy of Nature. You will find that your senses begin to get keener, as does your sense of color.

We limit ourselves with the few senses we use on a daily basis. Opening to Nature allows for many other senses to be available to us. The key is to practice allowing ourselves to be open to all that Nature and our environment has to offer us. Being stimulated by plant and flower colors is an example of allowing our senses to attune to shapes, colors, sizes, textures, and vibrations. These are qualities that we would not otherwise have sensed by using our mental, physical, spiritual, and natural gifts. It has to do with acceptance, with not putting learned limits on our experience of life.

While I was learning Indian Medicine I had many experiences that helped expand my realization that not everything is as we think it is, and there are things we don't understand, but it's alright. Acceptance is sometimes difficult when events do not fit our reason, perceptions, or logical thinking. My father was an electronics technician and television repairman. He taught me how to repair television sets and how to get the best signal for reception.

While working with one of the Cherokee Medicine Men, Doc Amoneeta Sequoyah, I noticed that his TV reception was very snowy and poor, which was par for the course in the mountains of North Carolina about thirty years ago. The elder said, "You know about getting the TV picture better, don't you? I bet you learned that from your father, didn't you?" Wanting to appear as though I really knew my stuff, I told him that I could take a field strength meter with the antenna up on the mountain and probably get a better picture, so we could watch football together.

On an early Sunday morning, in the dew and mist from a mountain rain, I came to his house loaded with my field strength meter, plenty of cable, and my tool pouch. I was ready to climb the mountain behind the elder's house to get him the perfectly snow-free picture. For hours I climbed up and down the mountain, slipping in mud and peat, determined to show him how much I had learned from my father about finding the best signal. After all, I had the latest electronic equipment to validate my findings, and I could verify the results with a strong signal reception and a snow-free picture on the television set. After several hours I was tired and hungry. The signal strength I had been looking for was just not there. I decided to come off the mountain and fix some bean soup for us to eat for lunch.

I must have been quiet in thought, trying to figure out what to do next. My mind went to the possibility of stringing the wire through the trees and using an amplifier to send the best signal down to the television set. As we slurped the soup the elder looked at me somewhat puzzled about what I was thinking. He said, "What is the meter telling you about the snow on the picture tube?" I paused as I got to the best part of the soup—the beans that had settled to the bottom of the bowl. "Well, I cannot find the strong signal that I thought I'd find on the mountain," I replied. He grinned as though he knew something I didn't and said, "Sometimes the meter don't always know something that the spirit ones know about these things." I was a little irritated and started to explain how the field strength meter worked. He seem intrigued and said, "Well, maybe the meter knows, but you are in the wrong place." I thought, just why had I been walking up and down that darn mountain to find the right place? That was what I was trying to do! Now I was even more determined to find that strong signal. I said I would continue my "work," and the elder just smiled. As I was walking to the door with my field strength meter he said, "Maybe you should just ask the Spirit Ones to work with you."

Once again I climbed the mountain, only to get the same results. Suddenly it started to rain, a soft mountain rain that sounded like many different drums as the water trickled on and off the leaves of the trees, increasing in rhythm. I quickly started down the mountain with my field strength meter in hand, concerned that the water would ruin the meter. Boy, then I would really be in trouble with my father, because I had removed the cover that he usually kept on the meter for protection. Approaching the house, I slipped in mud. The meter, the antenna, and I came sliding down until the antenna fell against the house, breaking one of its extensions. I sat there in the mud looking up at the elder, who had a smile on his face. He said, "You must have been in a hurry to decide to slide down the mountain. You should have seen what I saw. The antenna was a pullin' you one way and the meter was pullin' you the other way!" Rain was running down my face. We both laughed. He quietly said, "Why don't you come in, and let's watch the football game." With meter in hand, I slipped the ribbon cable from the antenna in through the window and came inside to dry off. To my surprise, when I connected the cable to the TV, the picture was snow-free! Well, not completely snow-free, but we still had a great picture! The elder looked at me and said, "Wonder what lesson you were to learn with all that?"

That was just the first of many lessons I would learn directly and indirectly as an apprentice in Indian Medicine. You could say that I was "in the beginning" of my many years of learning lessons of Indian Medicine and about the Spirit Ones. Several years later when the elder passed on, I went back up to the house where we had spent many wonderful teaching and laughing moments. Curious, I went around behind the house. There was the old antenna with a broken extension, resting awkwardly against a corner of the roof. I couldn't help shedding some tears like the raindrops of that fateful day—and laughing at the same time. I glanced at the window. For a split second I thought I saw Doc Amoneeta

Sequoyah looking back at me with a smile. I knew at that moment that I could always ask the Spirit Ones for guidance.

We can continue our journey into the world of Cherokee meditations by recalling that they are integral to an "Indian way of life," based on certain values. This way of life begins with a powerful energy that is pronounced "Na wah te." It is the flow of energy that is all life energy—the same energy that exists in Mother Earth. From an Indian perspective, Mother Earth is alive with an energy that also flows through us. She has a heartbeat. The flow of streams and rivers is like the flow of blood in our bodies. This energy is a healing energy. In essence, Mother Earth is our keeper of life, just as we are her protector. Everything exists in harmony and balance, in a definite pattern or within our circle of life. Harm to anything in that pattern of harmonic energy is harm to us as well.

East: Direction of Beginnings

Meditation for returning to the beginning focuses on the direction of the East. This direction represents family, group, togetherness, sharing, and spiritual connection. A certain freedom occurs in a family or group of friends who experience a sense of belonging and unity. This becomes a protection while you are on a spiritual journey. Any activity focused on sharing and connection satisfies our natural sense of fulfillment. Without this connection, we tend to feel somewhat lost and that we are missing something in our lives.

The symbol of the Sun in this direction was traditionally perceived as a power sign. The Sun ensured success in planting food for survival during the cold winter months in the mountains. Even today, canning food and preparing for the winter months is a routine activity. The meditation in this direction is focused on preparing for the future and obtaining protection in the group for the family, clan, and tribe. East is also the direction for honoring the elders and celebrating the beginning of new life.

The spirit connection in the direction of the East is the bird—the hawk or the eagle. Messages can come to you from the Bird-spirit world. In the Cherokee way of thinking, a feather lying in your path is a message. It is often a sign that something special will come to you. The omen is positive; it may foretell of something that is going to lead you to fly away from this path. It could also be a message for you to share with someone else, where you become the messenger.

I received such a message one day as I was driving across the bridge to Beaufort, North Carolina. A seagull came very close to the top of my car. I have a sunroof, so I could see it just over me. It seemed to be following me. As I came off the bridge to the street, another seagull flew right in front of me. Then I came too close to another auto parked on this narrow road, headed to the waterfront. This made me think I should just take a short break and think about things. I got a cup of coffee, sat down by the waterfront, and enjoyed watching the light bounce off the subtle movements of the water. A feather from a seagull fell right in front of me. I sat and meditated to see whether a picture would come to me. The only thing that came was "button down the hatch." I had a friend who had recently passed over to the other world, whose Indian name was Seagull (or Sea Eagle, as I called him). He loved walking on the beach and feeling the freedom of the seagulls. I kept thinking there was some connection between him and the seagulls and the feather.

A few days after this unusual event with the seagulls, I was preparing to travel west for a meeting in Asheville, North Carolina. Just to be safe, I buttoned down the hatch and put everything movable in the garage. I knew we had some strange weather patterns around us, with the possibility of a hurricane in the distance. During my meeting, Hurricane Dennis hit the North Carolina coast, causing enormous damage and flooding. One thing I had done before leaving was to set up the public health disaster plan for Carteret County with the assignments and equipment needed, just in case. No one could have known that this hurricane could flood the area with such destruction. Homes that had not been flooded in anyone's memory were covered in water. That was not all.

A few days later, on the tail of Hurricane Dennis, came the greatest disaster to hit eastern North Carolina in many years: Hurricane Fran. In every way possible, I put out the word to prepare and button down the hatch! The disaster and destruction left water above hundreds of homes and businesses. We were prepared with a team to go out and help people in need, but even with our preparations, we had no idea of how bad this could really be. The seagulls were probably trying to give many of us messages of a foretold disaster. Of course, it could also have just been coincidence. I accept both truths.

One of the lessons in the direction of the East is to accept all that comes to you, then choose what is comfortable for you. One of the meditations for the East is to be connected with the circle of close friends and family for protection, then to keep yourself free for choice.

The color associated with this direction is red, or sometimes gold or yellow. Red represents the power of the East and the Sun.

The color of the rising or setting sun with its brilliant colors must have been impressive for the early Cherokee. Red was also the color flown by the war chief. Ironically, this was also the color of life and the power color of the female, who had a definite influence in this direction with the circle of family, children, and clan involvement. Red was often the color representing fire, which of course was also associated with the beginning in Cherokee stories and myths.

In The Beginning: Fire

Today, the flame burning at the Mountainside Theater in Cherokee, North Carolina, is symbolic of the ceremonial fire. It is called the Eternal Flame. The early Cherokee associated fire with the elders in the culture. They called it the "ancient one," or sometimes the "old woman." The elders had the task of gathering wood for the fire in the family/clan or township. There was always a "beloved man" who would be the fire keeper at the traditional council house. Sometimes the elders referred to the fire as the beginning, calling fire Ancient Red or Grandfather. (The female aspect of fire, fire as old woman or Grandmother, associates fire with the nurturing quality of giving warmth, while the male aspect, or fire as Grandfather, acknowledges fire's qualities of strength and protection.)

When fire made its entrance in the creation, the Sun was born; therefore, fire and Sun were power symbols that were used at games or "little war." The color white, or Ancient White, refers to old age or wisdom and peace. One elder mentioned that the color yellow was also used with the fire, as that would be the color seen when burning certain woods. Although I could not find any reference to these colors in my research with the Cherokee Historical Association, I can accept the oral history from the elders.

In the meditation of fire, participants sit around the fire during the drumming and singing of songs. One elder said that fire was such a strong part of our ancestry that all we have to do is just imagine the sacred fire, and the entire scene will come to us. The last meditation in this chapter is for us to call on Grandmother Fire to warm our hearts and spirit. Call on the Great One in giving thanks for Sun, for a warm spirit. Recognize that the presence of fire represents a coming together that recalls for us the beginning of life here on Mother Earth. This can be done at any time, day or night: we can call on healing with warmth, knowledge, and understanding, and honor our elders because they gave us life in the beginning.

The meditation creates a feeling of coming together into a circle with friends in human, animal, and Nature, or "E lo he no." This coming together, or "Da ne la weh gah," is sacred. Whereas other meditations incorporate plants or flowers, in this meditation you will imagine or get into all of Nature. There you can feel the sense of this special harmony, the relationship of unity with all living things within the circle. The meditation is based on a basic set of values about the circle of life:

- There is one energy, all-inclusive and connected to the Great One (by whatever name you prefer to use).
- Medicine is a way of life based on the teachings of our ancestors. All belief systems have a similar basis, but the term *Medicine* includes the physical things around us, our mental and creative thoughts, the natural environment within our circle, and the spiritual energy that is life. Medicine also includes everything past and future as

being with us now in our "bundle" and connected to all other things.

- The sense of belonging starts with the beginning of time and continues through our ancestors to the connection we still have with family, clan, and tribe.
- There is equality in all things. Everything has its own purpose, and all things are equal. There is no such thing as dominance or control by any living thing over any other. There is basically only one relationship in the circle of life. We are to be humble and show humility to all things here on Mother Earth, even every rock and mineral.
- There are special people who are keepers of wisdom: chiefs, clan mothers, and others, depending on the tribe. They carry knowledge of everyday skills, of hunting and survival, of Medicine, of fire and herbal remedies. These are special gifts that have always been honored and respected. There have even been keepers of the traditions and teachings, who protected and shared them as appropriate in ceremonies.
- Nature's lessons can be learned by everyone according to their own gifts and individual lessons to be learned. For everything and every experience, there is a reason. Everything has its own life and a life hereafter. We belong to Nature's plan and have a special feeling and caring for Mother Earth. She provides for us and we protect her. You will hear this theme over and over in this book.
- Respect was and still is a part of our meditation and is shown by giving thanks for everything in our life circle.

Words are to be spoken with caution and care. We do not speak anything that would cause harm or consequence to the individual, family, or clan. Self-control and self-discipline are expected.

The meditation of the beginning as a way of life is as follows.

Find a comfortable place to sit, inside or outside. You may want to cover yourself in your favorite throw or blanket. Relax and breathe at least seven deep breaths, focusing on your belly moving in and out. Then imagine that you have a covering of energy around your entire body.

Put your hands close to your face and body to feel the energy and heat coming off your body. Feel the exchange of energy from your hands and your body as it goes both ways. You may even feel a little tingling in your hands and on your skin. Rest your hands on your lap as you focus inward.

At this moment, feel the inward calm of relaxation that surrounds you. Notice that you are in control of your own sensations of heat and coolness. You can choose to feel either one. Imagine a small breeze warming or cooling your body. Again, feel the control you have over your body and mind. You are experiencing the First Circle of Life: your body, mind, and spirit.

Now experience the Second Circle of Life, which extends beyond you as far as your hands will reach. Extend your hands out in front of you, and feel the energy move from within you to your fingertips. Then move your hands and arms in a circular motion to either side. Feel the energy as you move your hands back to your lap.

Continue to relax as you now focus on the Third Circle of Life. With your body completely relaxed, continue to breathe slowly. Open your energy at your head level, sometimes called the "third eye" at your forehead. Allow energy to come into you, and direct energy out of you. You are a receiver and a transmitter of energy. Notice the control you have over this process without even trying to do any conditioning. This is a natural process.

For now, simply close down the energy that comes in from outside, and relax. This is a closed energy exercise for the first three Circles of Life.

If you want to continue this process, open yourself to the Fourth Circle of Life. Open your energy by opening your hands and asking your spirit animal or guide to come to you for messages. Protect your energy by saying that only the energy or guide that will work *with* you will come in. Be firm in stipulating that only Good Medicine energy will come into your energy space. Keep your hands open in your lap.

To close the energy, simply turn your hands over. To have totally closed energy and complete protection, place your hands together by clenching them. Alternatively, just put your fingers together, or put your palms entirely together, pointing your fingers downward.

Continue to practice this meditation, opening and closing your hands, to feel the sense of self-control and self-healing. The objective is to learn the self-control of being able to relax and open your hands to feel the sense of open spirit and energy; then to be able to turn your hands over to close down the energy, or shut it off like a switch, for deeper relaxation and healing.

In the next chapter we will celebrate life and focus more on the Universal Circle of all life.

2

CEREMONY OF LIFE

For the Cherokee, every day is a special and sacred day. This was true for the early Cherokee in the planting fields or with a hunting party, and it is just as true today for a Cherokee living and working in this hi-tech world. Some things just do not change. One of them is the appreciation of Mother Earth and all that Nature has to provide, which the Cherokee still revere and respect today as they did hundreds of years ago. In those earlier years, land and resources were plentiful. Today, the scarcity of land and resources is a continuing issue. Our work and living conditions put us almost continuously into proximity to electrical currents and vibrations. While our body will adjust to these different vibrations, the interference causes us to become tired more easily than if we were outside in Nature. That is why it is so important that we have some time every day in our natural environment, outside of our homes, cars, and workplaces. As one elder put it, "We must touch Mother Earth each day. My father worked every day outside as a logger with a crew. When he came home each day, he would take off his boots and walk on Mother Earth with his bare feet. He would say that it felt good to have the energy of our Earth Mother coming into his feet when he walked as a free man. He remembered his father coming home from the boarding school and taking off his shoes to run and walk. I prefer to just sit on Mother Earth."

The Sacred Seven

The ceremony of life begins by understanding the importance of the number seven, which is a sacred number to the Cherokee. While we really do not know its origin, the elders have expressed it as relating to the four cardinal directions along with the upper world, the lower world, and the center. The center, or fire, is the beginning. Its connection to the Great One has been described as an invisible cord. At birth we move into the direction of the East toward the light.* Our cycle brings us into the world with our first breath, with little attention given to the light in the beginning.

Once we exist as a life force or human being, we consider that we have life. Ironically, the early Cherokee teachers viewed birth

---

*It intrigued me to hear that turtle hatchlings know to move toward the light of Grandmother Moon, which takes them to the water for survival. Many people have expressed concerns about the artificial lights put in parking areas so that tourists can enjoy the oceanfront at night. The turtle hatchlings will follow the direction of the streetlights and eventually expire.

as the beginning of afterlife, and our commitment and purpose on Mother Earth is to serve life, both now and after death. Therefore, every action and reaction had a consequence that affected not only the individual but the family, clan, and tribe. The seven festivals or ceremonies of the early Cherokee focused on more than a ceremony of life here on Mother Earth. They included our commitment to the ancestors, our elders, and the little ones who would eventually guide us in their adulthood. The key concept was guidance from the ancestors, the spirit world, and all that represented the Great One, the Universal Spirit.

The Cherokee have always known that we are a part of a greater unity extending back to the beginning of life and into the future of life. Life itself was considered beautiful, which meant that we would show our gratitude with ceremony, song, dance, and feasts of sharing with every form of life.

In addition to the key concept of guidance, there was a sense of respect for everything. Everything had a purpose, and every purpose was related to helping and protecting Mother Earth and all its inhabitants. Nothing was taken for granted, nor was anything neglected in the ceremony of life. Can you imagine what an honor it must have been to be part of this sacred existence, which methodically gave thanks for everything, every day? One of those thankgivings each day was for female energy and for life itself. The female spirit gives life, and that life is celebrated and honored.

Honoring Female Energy

John Howard Payne recorded some of the ways in which the early Cherokee showed honor and respect for female energy, which was identified with maize or Indian corn and always received special honor in ceremonies such as the Green Corn Festival. Payne also noted that she was considered the "woman of the East." This honor meant that she was the beginning and the beginning-again of life itself! What an honor to bestow on a human being! Corn represented woman as the mother of a child, as the grandmother guiding the child and the adult, and as the spirit that gave us life, in the form of the staple food that sustains life itself, called "Selu" in the Cherokee language.

The ceremony of life begins with the origin of the first fire. In the beginning there was darkness and no fire. The Great One sent the Thunder Beings to bring life to Mother Earth. The new Earth was cold, and Sun had just started to heat the land during what we now know as day. Still, the nights were cold, as Moon's task was to protect us and to slowly start the germination of seeds for trees and plants on this new island called Mother Earth. One of the sacred trees to come to this new land was Sycamore; many others, such as Oak and Pine would come later. Some of the trees, such as Redbud and Cherry Tree, were eager to come to this new land, but they had to wait because they needed much light to bloom and to create fruit for the animals.

The Thunder Beings sent their lightning to put fire at the bottom of a sycamore tree that was on a small island in the water by itself. All the animals saw the smoke, but they were not sure how to bring the fire back to their tribal council. The animals met in council and decided that all the animals that could swim or fly would go and bring the fire back to council. First to make the trip was Raven. He was a beautiful large bird with white feathers until he flew over the sycamore tree, where fire and smoke rose high in the sky. Raven could not land on the tree, and his feathers became scorched and black. He returned without the fire. The same thing happened to Owl, who got his eyes blackened with the hot smoke as he looked into a hollow part of the tree. To this day, members of the Owl tribe have rings around their eyes, and they have trouble seeing, except at night.

It was decided that the Snake tribe would swim to the island. First was little Racer Snake, "Uksu hi," who got close to the burning fire. He was blinded by the hot ashes, and his body was scorched black. Ever since, the racer snake has darted back and forth as if trying to get away from the fire. The same thing happened to Blacksnake, or "Gule gi."

Finally, little Water Spider said that she would quickly move across the water and weave a "Tus ti" bowl to carry a hot coal on her back. The council agreed. Thus, Water Spider brought the fire to the First Council on Mother Earth, and she is always honored in ceremonies that recall that first fire. Fire is held sacred by the Cherokee, and it is always in the center of the Sacred Circle in ceremonies.

The ceremony of life is a time to clear our ways for a fresh start with each new moon as we celebrate friendships and life itself. It is a time to make things right or to follow the traditional way of right relationship. The fire is a reminder that we must go back to the center and celebrate life as our focus in meditation. In sharing warmth and energy with others we establish and maintain the way of right relationship in the Universal Circle. We can renew our respect for life in many ways:

- Respect life, all life! Do something to be a helper to life. Plant a plant or a tree to see it grow and produce life. Maybe you can save a turtle from the highway, or a bird that has fallen from the nest. Maybe you can be a helper to a child or an elder who needs your assistance to sustain life or to improve the quality of life.
- Celebrate life by recognizing someone's birthday or a beginning. Your gesture can be as simple as a card to say thanks, or just your presence for a friend who may be in need. You might share a candle with someone as a symbol of the first fire to celebrate life and being alive. The key is to share with humility and to show respect for others.
- Show respect and honor to someone with a small amount of tobacco, which is considered sacred by Native Americans. This is not to smoke but to remind us that the tobacco, like sage and cornmeal, is shared with the ceremonial fire to send a message to the Great One. Sharing some tobacco is done, even today, as a way to ask permission or to give thanks.

Have you ever thought about how special it is to share a fire with others in a circle? The fire can be as simple as a candle burning in a room of friends spending time together, or as elaborate as a sacred powwow fire at an intertribal gathering. Throughout the history of American Indians and Alaska Natives, the sharing of a fire has been so sacred that only certain woods would be used, and only certain trained persons would be Keepers of the Fire. Even the ashes of such a ceremonial fire would be shared as a reminder of this great event, to recall for everyone the ceremony of life and the Universal Circle of Life.

On one of my trips to Oklahoma to visit an Indian Medicine teacher there, I had a chance to attend a stomp dance, a ceremony I was not very familiar with. There was a wonderful formality about the Cherokee men in traditional dress and the women with long colorful dresses. Chills ran up and down my arms. I had been invited by Archie Sams, a Natchez-Cherokee, to visit the Cherokee Nation and to see a stomp dance. I was fascinated by the women in traditional dress, wearing turtle shells strapped to their legs. The turtle shells rattled as the women danced around in the circle. The women were very powerful in their dance. I was absolutely hypnotized by the sound and the movement as if the dance had struck some inner or spirit part of me. Not only did it remind me of our Fall Festival, but the energy and sacredness were extremely potent.

Writing now about my experience at the stomp dance in Oklahoma almost twenty years ago, I can still hear the song-chant. The drum beat and the movement of the turtle rattles strapped to the women's legs made a continuous beat with the song, "Hi yo wi go hue le, hyo hi ya we . . . Ho hi yo wa he, Ha Ha Yo." It was one of the most wonderful experiences I have ever had at a ceremonial dance.

One of the elders was explaining how to stomp dance to a young one. He said, "Ya' gotta just pretend that you are moving slowly to stomp on a bunch of ants that are moving away from you. Ho Hi Ya Wa He, just feel the rhythm and stomp on those ants." I started to laugh because I could just see these little ants scurrying to get away from the dancer's moccasins. The elder saw me laughing and said, "Maybe you want to try it so we can laugh at you." I hesitated and told him I was from Cherokee, North Carolina, and I was just imagining the ants scurrying around and myself getting all mixed up and falling on my face. He started to laugh with me. After a few minutes, we connected as he told me of his distant family, named Squirrel, back in my home. He and I danced, and every once in a while he would look at me and say, "Have you stepped on any ants yet?"

Truly, a ceremony of life was going on at the stomp dance in Oklahoma as I visited with my Cherokee Nation brothers and sisters. The old Cherokee ceremonies include all members of the family, clan, and tribe in the activities. Everyone participates, from the youngest to the oldest. It was truly inspiring to see all the little ones in traditional dress, enjoying their uniqueness as Native Americans and as Cherokee Indians.

One of my lessons was about the Old Ones, as ancestors and as teachers of the traditions. When the old folks' dance was called, the elders gladly came up to the dance circle. Twenty times they danced around in a slow fashion to the sounds of the drum and rattles, chanting "Hi Yo Ho, Hi Yo Ho," until they shouted "Hwu." I joined them at the request of an elder. By the time I was finished, my "Hwu" was more like a "Whew!" But instead of being tired, those Oklahoma elders seemed to be more energized. They were laughing and thoroughly enjoying the social togetherness.

The lesson I learned was about the importance of ceremony in the lives of tribal folks all over America. The energy and power of women became much clearer to me when I saw the women stomping with their turtle shells and the older women dancing in the old folks' dance. Whatever touched me in this event made me show more respect and honor to women from that time forward. I realized something sacred about the role of women and their energy in the ceremony of life, about the role of women in maintaining the circle of life.

The celebration and ceremony of life with traditional dance, drumming, and songs are truly powerful, whether among Akaska Natives in the North or the Pasqua Yaqui in the South; the intertribal groups in the Indian country of Oklahoma, or the Cherokee in the East. We need to find that common ground for coming together, feasting, and celebrating life for all people, all over the world.

In my tobacco prayers and offerings to the sacred fires at every ceremony, powwow, and celebration with American Indians and Alaska Natives, I ask that we find a way to have a coming-together to celebrate life in our own cultural and traditional ways in the Universal Circle for all people in the world, for peace, harmony, and balance.

Ceremony of Life

A Cherokee elder once told me of this event in his youth. "I was just a little boy. There was a gathering in Big Cove, where there was more food than I had ever seen. It was a celebration honoring the passing of someone I really cannot even remember, I was so young. There was a young girl there who had kicked my butt before. You know, Cherokee women are nothing to mess with when they get their dander up. Before this I would show her how many fish I could catch up at Twin Forks, or how I could drum. This night was a long one, but the old one who had passed used to teach the dances. He wanted everyone to dance, sing, and eat plenty of food. While I cannot remember the young girl's name now, because I am an old man myself, I watched her dance. She had the turtle rattles tied to her like they used to do. I heard the beat of the rattles and the drum. Even though there was lots going on, I could hear the rattling of the turtle rattles. I started to sing my own song. Suddenly the girl caught my eyes, so I looked down real quick." The elder wiped a tear from his eye and continued to tell his story.

"A feeling came over me that I can still feel today when I think about that special time. You see, you didn't dance at a wake, but remember—this old one had taught all us young people the sacred dances and songs. He was one of a kind, because most people were getting away from the old ways. From that time on, I followed that little girl whenever I could. Of course, she could not see me because I would hide—well, so I thought. When we were older, she told me that she always knew I was there. Sometimes when I saw her, I still had that picture in my mind of her dancing with the turtle rattles. That is where I got the special song that I sing today. Well, that was a long time ago. I've been married to that woman more years than I can remember. You see, the woman has a power greater than us men can understand. We must respect that power and be glad they are with us and are not using it against us, because we would surely be in trouble. The point is that they are the ceremony of life."

The Cherokee elder continued with his song-chant and rattle. I could vividly see the little girl in a long flowing traditional dress, her turtle shells rattling with the beat of the drum. I could also hear the soft sound of the corn moving inside the turtle rattles, and I sensed the spirit of the ancestors there with us. Wa do (Skee)!

Ceremony of Life and the Universal Circle

In April 1984, at Red Clay, Tennessee, the Cherokee Nation in Oklahoma and the Eastern Band of Cherokee Indians came together to reunite for the first time since the Trail of Tears in 1838. Then, several thousands of Cherokee were forcibly gathered at Red Clay to begin the long trip to Indian territory in Oklahoma. Now there is a historic park, which symbolizes the coming together and the lighting of the torch that was carried eastward by Indian runners from Qualla Boundary to Red Clay. The sacred flame was returned to the place where there is to be a healing of our past.

The meditation to renew our coming together is for you the reader to contact everyone that has ever helped you and thank them. The exercise is clearing and healing. Even for those that have already gone on to the spirit world, just meditate quietly in a special place to thank them for being a helper. To end this meditation and to begin again, be a helper to others in the Universal Circle and the Ceremony of Life.

Ceremony of Life Meditation

The meditation of life is about light, or "U la sa tah." The ceremonies of the Sun were about life as being transparent, like the quartz crystal. The early Cherokee enjoyed celebrating life and Nature. As an elder put it, "Early Cherokee were still like children, before they met the white man. While serious about life, they were also serious about play. They did a lot of things to develop the curious mind, such as hide and seek, or find how many different leaves there are from here to there. We have forgotten these simple games about life." We can practice experiencing Nature in meditation, or meditating in Nature to develop our senses about life.

The early Cherokee honored knowledge and skill. This was to honor the family, clan, and tribe, but not the individual. As an elder said, "I practiced becoming the best double-weave basket maker in the tribe. People would see my basket and know it was one of my baskets. It was so tight that it would hold water. People would say that I had a gift. Regardless of how hard I worked to learn this old skill of basket making, they would still say that I had the gift, or I was gifted by the Great One to do this thing, and that's OK, because they knew who made the basket." The elder was proud to let me know that all his hard work had finally resulted in a basket that would give his family, clan, and tribe honor as basket weavers. In the Cherokee tradition, the person is respected for his or her skill, but the honor goes to the tribe.

Practice this meditation to learn how to protect your mind and communicate with the spirit world. Before beginning this meditation for the Ceremony of Life, recall that you have already experienced the first four Circles of Life. Now you are ready for the Fifth Circle of Life, which goes back to the center of the fire, to your own spirit or soul.

First, get into a comfortable place in Nature or inside a warm protected place. Do this alone or in a circle group with someone guiding the journey, perhaps interacting with the others. You can sit or stand in the circle. You can also move to other spots to meditate, then return to the circle.

The next step is to continue deep breathing and

relaxation while you focus on creating a harmonic energy around you that is totally calm. Remember that calm is also healing. Close your eyes. You are in a special place in the woods or near a mountain stream. This is a warm and beautiful day. You can smell the scent of flowers and peppermint. You can hear the birds sing and chirp as they live their lives and feed on Nature's bountiful food supply. There is a slight breeze in the air, not too cool or too warm. Listen to the water flowing in the stream, to the breeze rustling the leaves on the trees. Remember that Mother Earth has special gifts for all of us. Realize that the colors before our eyes are all the colors of Nature.

Take several long, deep breaths of fresh air as you feel your belly protrude, then suck in your belly as you slowly exhale. Keep your breathing slow and relaxed. Feel the sense of being happy in this moment. Be thankful for all these gifts of Nature, for being Nature's child. Smile gently like the Sun to let Nature see your calm and healing smile.

Now open your energy, knowing you are fully protected, to the Fifth Circle of Life—to all the energy that surrounds you in the four cardinal directions. Practice focusing on the sounds, the breeze, and the special messages of birds, animals, and plants. Ignore man-made sounds that may intrude, and focus on Nature's harmonic energy. It is relaxing and healing.

In this Fifth Circle, your spirit connects with the spirit of all things around you. You are not limited by your own energy space, but you can project outward and upward to feel everything going on for as far as you want to feel. You are connected in spirit to the spirit world around you and to that which you cannot see with your physical eyes. You are part of an ancient culture and connected to your ancestors. In this meditation you have opened your spirit to the Ceremony of Life.

Our next journey will take us to the Green Corn and our connection with Mother Earth.

3

GREEN CORN

Corn was considered sacred by the early Cherokee. Life was focused on survival, and ceremony gave thanks for this food of life. The summer months, or "go gi," started with the first full moon in April with a ceremony called "a dan wisi" to recognize the time of planting. This was a busy time for planting corn and other crops in preparation for the next winter. The end of this planting cycle was in August, the time of the Green Corn Feast of "se lu," when the roasting of corn would celebrate life. In the middle of September, all the clans would come together for another Green Corn Feast, this of one "don ago huni," the maturity of corn. The Old Woman of the spirit of corn is "Agaw' la." A very old story tells of how she gave her life for the sons of the Cherokee to have corn for survival, as long as they worked in the planting fields to plant corn. There are several Cherokee stories about corn. This is one story I remember well.

Grandmother Selu was raising a small boy. His parents were away on a long trip that would take them far away from the Smoky Mountains for many moons. Each day, Little Boy went into the planting field as Grandmother prepared the hard ground for planting corn, beans, and squash. She would rake the ground with a stick to soften the ground. Sometimes she would call to the worms in the earth to be helpers for the seeds to rest in soft soil for germination. Little Boy would watch her do Medicine as she sang an old Cherokee song, one that has been lost with the passing of the moons. Each evening they went to the cabin, where she started a fire to boil the corn or roast it for the evening meal.

Often Little Boy went to gather kindling for the fire while Grandmother Selu said that she had to go to the corn bin for corn to cook. She always said, "Little Boy, you gather the wood for the fire, and I will collect the corn from the storage bin." He was told to stay away from the bin where the corn was kept because of a snake that fed on fallen corn around the storage bin. It seemed strange to him that he never saw Grandmother Selu carry corn from the field to the storage bin, but she always had beans in a basket and tomatoes from the planting field. She always brought the corn back in a long apron, which she then wore over her dress while she prepared the food for their evening meal.

One day near the time when the Sun was at rest and darkness was near, Little Boy decided to follow Grand-

mother Selu and hide in the high bushes near the
storage bin. To his amazement, she did not even open
the bin but just rubbed her hands as she held the apron
open. Golden yellow corn would appear in her apron!
Little Boy was so surprised that he immediately said,
"Grandma Selu, how did you do that!" Startled, she
turned to him with a look of stars in her eyes and said
that now she would have to go away forever. He
suddenly felt sad. Grandmother Selu fixed the corn for
their evening meal, and later she held him, explaining
that some things are not to be seen. The next morning
when Little Boy awoke to the bright morning light, his
aunt was there to stay with him. Grandmother Selu was
never to be seen again, but in the fields were rows and
rows of golden yellow corn ready to be picked from the
large stalks. Little Boy sang the song he remembered
hearing her sing as she planted the corn, which the
Cherokee call Selu.

My grandfather said that we must to save seven ears of corn from
the harvested crop to preserve until the new crop was ready for
harvest. According to an old tale, one should not blow on the
new corn that was eaten at the Green Corn dance because it would
cause a windstorm to blow down the corn stalks in the planting
fields. My grandfather also told me that in the old days, seven
corn grains were put into each hill at planting. A special song-
chant and wailing would be done to symbolize the Old Woman's
gift of her blood so that the people could have corn. Earlier Green
Corn rituals of harvesting and planting were sacred and included
the elder priests.

The early Cherokee planted other crops as regular staple foods.

Beans, or "tu ya," especially kidney beans, are still a favorite food. Pumpkins, or "i yah" and varieties of squash, or "wa tsi gu," are also included as food staples of the Cherokee today.

Along with the foods, the early Cherokee cultivated tobacco for ceremonies and Medicine. Tobacco, *Nicotiana rustica,* was called "Tsa lu," which originally referred to fire. Tobacco would be given to the main fire during ceremonies to give thanks and send a message to the Great One. This ritual of giving and even smoking tobacco was considered sacred in the New Fire Ceremony in October and November. In the earliest Cherokee story, of the beginning of the world, only one tobacco plant was taken by the wild goose. Different animals tried in vain to get the tobacco back, but only the humming bird succeeded.

Little People Celebration

Green Corn Ceremony celebrates the harvest of corn, beans, squash, and tobacco along with many other plants and herbs to prepare for the cold winter. It is also a time to remind us of the Little People and the role they play in our lives. Some Cherokee say Little People are spirit people; others describe them as very real people who are about three feet tall. One of the elders told me a story when we visited Ellijay Creek, near Franklin, North Carolina. He was looking for certain herbs that were considered sacred to the Burning Town settlement of the Cherokee in earlier days. Similar to yellow root, the plant had a medicinal purpose: it was used for settling the stomach and also for parasites. He said that the Cherokee Little People, called "Yunwi Tsunsdi," were real people who had lived in the mountains since long before the Cherokee came there. He described seeing some of them one evening when he could conceal himself. He was on a journey to search for a sacred herb, at one of the original settlements of the early Cherokee, thought to be a sacred place. There he saw the Little People about fifty feet in front of him, down at the edge of a creek, gathering a plant that looked like yellow root.

A young man apprenticing in the Medicine at the time, he wanted to get closer to them. The man had heard of the Little People but did not believe they were real. He thought that they might be dwarf people or just short people seen from a distance. He crept quietly through the thick woods to get a closer look. The Little People were dancing, and they had long hair that almost reached the ground. He thought, "What a time not to have someone else with me to see this. How will I describe this to anyone?" He could hear a drum beating, although he could not see anyone playing the drum. The Little People danced as they pulled the bark from the plant and put it into a deerskin bag. "Why the bark—why not the roots, as I am familiar with using?" he thought to himself. He wondered whether they used it as a medicinal herb or in some ceremony. He decided to follow them.

When the Little People had gathered enough of the thin bark from the sacred plant to fill their small Medicine bags, they went dancing into the night. The elder telling the story said that he followed them to a cave that seemed to appear out of the night sky. It was a real cave, but he could not remember having seen it in this place, even though he had roamed there frequently as a young boy, fishing and looking for arrowheads. He could not see into the caves, and decided to come back in the daylight without telling anyone of his venture. When he returned, he saw the thin strips of bark near a large locust tree near the mountainside, but could not find the cave he had seen the night before. Lying under the bark were some beautiful clear crystals, much like the ones found near Grandfather Mountain. They seemed to just be sticking in the ground. He knew he should not move or touch them, for fear of making the Little People angry at him.

Each fall at the change of the season, he would travel back to the same creeks to see if he could find some of the beautiful crystals lying on the ground. To my surprise, when I accompanied him, I did find a clear quartz crystal near one Ellijay creek. On the bank were some beautiful plants called yellow Indian shoe, or yellow moccasin. Most people know the plants as lady's slipper, which are about two feet tall and have a yellow saclike flower. This plant was often used as a mild sedative to help someone sleep, though it is not used much today. In the wet area near one of the small creeks was a plant that I knew as twinleaf, or rheumatism root. The leaves resemble a butterfly, and it is quite different from yellow root.

While the elder and I could still not understand how the strips of thin bark were used with the quartz crystals, we were reminded of the many different plants that were called yellow root. Were the Little People teaching us both something about the Medicine? Green Corn Ceremony is a time to share what has been learned about the plants and food that help us all—a time for the Medicine Men and Medicine Women to share their teachings with younger apprentices in Cherokee Medicine. Whether the Little People are real or we see them in spirit, I believe they have taught us much about medicinal plants and about the uses of sacred stones that we use in our ceremonies even today.

Green Corn Ceremony

The Green Corn Ceremony was held in August. Corn was not to be eaten until after this special event. Every year, seven ears of corn were taken by special runners who were trained as Deer Riders. For this ceremony, the special runner would take the seven ears of corn to the chief of the "center town." At that time, the chief and his seven helpers, or counselors, would fast for six days, and the ceremony would begin on the seventh day. The sacred fire would be started by the Fire Keepers. The chief would take seven kernels of corn from each of the seven ears and place them in the fire as he gave thanks to the Great One. Then he would share some tobacco with the fire. That was the signal for food to be prepared from corn brought by each clan and shared with everyone who participated as clan and tribe.

You can recall and honor the Green Corn Ceremony by planning a feast for the first new moon of August. Be sure to get at least seven ears of corn, and dry out seven kernels of corn to place in your Medicine bag. This is a reminder of how important corn and other food is to your survival. Cook the corn in your favorite way, or on the cob, and share this sacred food with your friends and family. This is also a time to think of what is needed to prepare for the long winter months. Fortunately, we can be safe in our warm homes, but we also need to plan for a time when we will be without electricity or will need to help others who may not have food and shelter during the cold winter days and nights.

Finding and Gifting

Green Corn Ceremony was traditionally a time to give thanks for the gifts of food. Even today, our Fall Festival celebrates the variety of canned and freshly grown foods, and the Cherokee give thanks to the Great One and Mother Earth for these special gifts of food, nutrition, and Medicine. Besides communicating with plants and the Little People in Green Corn Ceremony, we give thanks for the gifts we receive as we share tobacco prayers. We also gift to remind ourselves of the value of sharing. Despite the jokes about "Indian giving," Indian people are very generous. We do not value possessions as being primarily important, especially when it comes to friendships and commitments. Teaching young people this value early in life is very important to Indian families. It usually starts with the sharing of food, then items for play and gifting for the Medicine bag. When I was growing up I was particularly interested in the stories of gifts from the Little People. Some Cherokee elders say that the Little People leave us gifts of crystals and special stones in a manner that defies logic and normal understanding.

Once, while hiking in the mountains near Grandfather Mountain in North Carolina, I saw a shiny piece of wing-shaped metal sticking out from the ground. Strangly, although I was with a small group of young people, I was the only one who saw it. When I pulled it out, I recognized it as a pipe holder. It looked like silver but turned out to be an alloy. Where the bowl of a pipe would fit, it was almost a perfect carving of an eagle on a nest. When I told a Cherokee elder what had happened, she said that the Little People must have meant for me to find it. The item had probably been made in the early 1800s, so how did it get there on a hidden trail?

The elder explained that Little People find things that people have lost or left behind, then save them to gift someone.

Some thirty years later, when I had forgotten about the incident, I was working with a Cherokee Medicine Man. He had a pipe that he would set on the nightstand. One night it fell over and started a small fire. When he told me about it I remembered the pipe holder. As first I couldn't remember where I had put it; then suddenly there was a clear picture in my mind about where it was. I had put it in a very old green Ball jar that was gifted to me by a friend who had found it in an old home he was renovating. I got the pipe holder and gave it to the elder. He grinned and said, "The Little People must have gifted you with this." My jaw must have dropped a foot! "How did you know?" "Well, I have been given some unusual gifts like this from the Little People, and I always pass them along, in time, to someone who needs it," he said with a slight grin. "I hope you left something in return. It is the Good Medicine thing to do. I replied that I had. The only things I had in my pocket were a penny and a little heart-shaped rock that I wanted to give to a special girl. So I left the penny. My mother taught me to always leave something when Mother Nature gives you a special gift. Things always come full circle.

The Power of Food

Celebration with food is a powerful experience that equals none other. Ask any chef about the power of food—the preparation, the intensity of the delivery or presentation of food. All over the world, food is the centerpiece of great meetings and decisions. Food is a way to celebrate a coming-together of people. Food is also Medicine, besides being nutritious and the basis for good health. We have so many gifts of knowledge about food that have come from American Indians. In this book I want to share some of those gifts. Just to list a few, they include many berries, such as cranberries and blackberries which are used in pies and healing drinks. Squash, peanuts, persimmons, many varieties of beans and potatoes, and of course corn are all gifts of food to the Cherokee.

Indian tribes on Turtle Island had a vast knowledge of how to use the nutritional value of animal meats, fish, and plants for protein, mineral salts, fats, vitamins, and healing. The early Indian diet was very nutritious and healthy. Indian Medicine people had a tremendous knowledge of medicinal herbal remedies. A brew of spruce bark and needles was used to cure scurvy, and purple coneflower to rid the body of an infection. Many medicinal remedies were related to common foods. I grew up on corn, cornbread, beans, hominy, and many greens that were prepared to keep us healthy. The old way of roasting corn and soaking it in ashes mixed with water resulted in hominy, which was ground to make grits. Cornmeal was even mixed with small amounts of cedar ashes containing mineral salts to increase the nutritional value of breads. Acorns were eaten by the people of many Indian tribes. Somehow they learned to wash the acorns after pounding them to leach the bitter tannic acid. The flour was used for soups, and the oil was used as a seasoning. We now know of the health benefits of steaming vegetables. The idea came from the Indian practice of steaming shellfish in cane baskets filled with vegetables and water and placed on heated stones.

The Cherokee still make a stew of shrimp and okra, which was probably the original gumbo, a popular Louisiana dish. Beef cooked over an open fire with seasoning was probably the original barbecue. I do not know of any barbecue sauce created by the Cherokee, but I do suspect that the sauces came from Southwest tribes. The Choctaw Indians used many powders in sauces and stews. One that comes to mind was a powder that was pounded from sassafras leaves and dried in the sun. The Spanish learned how to tenderize meat from the Seminoles, who used papaya juice and pounded the meat to make it easier for the elderly to eat. Today, a substance in the papaya fruit is used as an active ingredient in meat tenderizers.

Lessons from Green Corn

It is my hope that the reader will never look at an ear of corn again without associating it with the elder woman Selu. The sacrifice of hard work and toil to plant, grow, and harvest our food should be good reason to thank our farmers for the gift of food. We are to eat slowly and give thanks for the nutritious and healing qualities of food as we share this special time with family and friends.

Many lessons for life can be learned from planting and growing food. Young people can learn discipline by working in the fields or in a garden. As a youngster, I had the chore of cutting down and preparing the planting area. I spent many hours raking out stones and finding broken arrowheads and pieces of pottery. The rows went from north to south, with the tallest plants on the north and east sides of the field. The early crops of lettuce, peas, and spinach were sown first, then space was made for crops such as tomatoes and peppers for the hot season. Succession planting began with early lettuce, followed by carrots or radishes, then beets. There was a design to our planting. Corn and beans shared the same space so that the bean plants could climb the corn stalks.

The elders said to me, "Sowing the seeds for food is the same as sowing the seeds of life. If you do not have a plan and discipline yourself to that plan, you will end up in trouble with a young lady and your life." In the planting field there was time for families to talk about what was going on as everyone worked together. Preparing and planting the fields for food was a family time. We referred to this time as a time for planting seeds that will be food for our bodies, and it was also a time for the adults and teachers to plant "spirit" seeds in us for the "food of life." Some of my fondest memories of my father are of our working in the garden. As a young boy I also had some wonderful conversations with my mother about life when we planted flowers. One of the most difficult things for me to do was to thin out the plants. I really hated to see any of them be pulled and left to go back to Mother Earth without seeing their plant life come to fruition. I also realized that unless the seedlings were thinned, the radishes would not form bulbs. I learned that lesson the hard way. Some of my carrots did not grow, and the lettuce did not produce when it was crowded. The elders said, "You are learning that there is a reason for everything we do. We learn these things from our ancestors so we don't make the same mistakes. Such is life itself. Always listen to the wisdom of the elders. They understand life."

The food of life was also the food of spirit. Yes, I said the food of spirit. I was sowing the seeds of warmth-loving plants that included tomatoes, peppers, and cucumbers. The elder told me to remember the lima beans. They were to be planted two inches apart and one inch deep in rows that were two feet apart. Of course, that included the baby lima beans, which we called butter beans. I learned that if limas blossom in the hottest part of the summer, they may not set beans. Actually, the pod will devour the seeds within; therefore, planting early can help. I was also planting snap beans, beets, broccoli, cabbage, carrots, celery, cucumbers, corn, collards, okra, onions, parsnips, peas, peppers, potatoes, radishes, squash, pumpkin, tomatoes, turnips, and rutabagas. I am getting hungry just listing these foods!

Before starting the planting season I forgot to plant the most important seeds of all: the sunflower seeds. Sunflowers protect the planting area and get the attention of the Sun's light first, which then awakens the other seed spirits. One elder told me that each seed has its own spirit, just like each one of us. Each seed had to be put into the ground with love and caring. An elder said to me, "The little seed can hear you, so speak only good words, and ask it to grow healthy and strong!" Any negative energy or anger would hurt the seeds and the entire planting field. He also said that we must always greet the young plants with a smile: "How are you doing today? What can I do to be a helper for you? Are you thirsty?" And at night, "Go to sleep so you can greet the light with a smile." I used to think this was pretty funny.

The elder told me of a time when he resented having to work in the garden while he could have been playing with his friends. In his hurry to sow the seeds, he forgot to plant the sunflower seeds. To the Cherokee, the sunflower is very special. There are several stories about these sacred sunflower seeds, this one made sense to me.

There are those who say that the sunflower seeds were brought to the Smoky Mountains by a stranger who carried a large pouch containing many kinds of beans and seeds from another place in the South. He had traded some furs for food to eat. When he discovered that these tiny oily seeds did not have any taste, he was upset. He tried to trade them with others, but they just laughed at him and said that even the Sun would not help the seeds to grow. He carried them to Cherokee country, where a group of hunters provided him food and warmth. The stranger forgot his pouch, which stayed lost in the woods for many months. In the late spring, before ceremony, some young Cherokee came upon these tall flowering plants that seemed to smile at them. They went quickly back to the village to share their story with others. Everyone wanted to see large flowers that smiled.

The keeper of seeds was an elder called Planter. He was summoned to go with the young Cherokee to retrieve the mysterious plant. The first thing he saw was the Sun shining directly on the plant, and the plant glowing bright yellow in the presence of the Sun. He took some of the seeds lying on the ground and cut one of the flowers to show the people. They were surprised at seeing such a big beautiful yellow flower that really smiled at them. They decided that this plant would please the Sun, so from that day forward they planted the seeds in the East of the planting field. Ever since, the Cherokee planting fields have yielded more food and more varieties of beans and corn, thanks to the sunflower.

Similar stories have been told by the Natchez, Creek, Seneca, and other American Indians about the sunflower and its value to planting. The elder telling me the story recalled a time when he forgot to plant the seeds of the sunflower as directed. When he found them in his pocket, he decided to just eat them. That year the planting field did not grow well at all, and there were so many storms that even the hardy corn was left lying in the fields that were too wet, then too dry. The elder said he never again forgot to plant the sunflower seed.

When you meditate on Green Corn, be aware of how your attitude affects your own spirit and the spirit of all the plants around you. Remember that the plants are your friends. Be kind to the plants and give thanks for the life they reproduce and the oxygen you have to breathe because of them. Remember also to share a smile with every flower and plant, for they share life and spirit connection with you.

4

SUN AND MOON

The ceremonial name for Sun in Cherokee is "Nu dah." Sometimes the elders spoke of the Sun as a mother who had a daughter, and the Moon was called the Grandmother. At other times the elders referred to the Sun as a sister to the Moon, or as our grandparents who deserve to be respected. One thing is for sure: the Sun has always been a focal point in ceremonies and in the Cherokee way of life as established by agriculture and planting seasons. The Sun was praised and thanked each day for the light. The light, or "ehi," provided an opening into the day, "ega." Each rising of the Sun was considered a great day, as though life had started all over again. There was always a feeling of gladness when the Sun rose in the morning. It was the time to do the chores and to celebrate life!

The Cherokee elder who shared stories about the Sun with me would always have me take him to a special place in the Smoky Mountains where the wildflowers were abundant. He would walk as quickly as he possibly could, as though he were going to see his old friends again. In his excitement, he would talk about seeing how much the little plants had grown since he was last there. He would talk to the plants. If he stepped on a little shoot or sprig of a plant, he would say, "Oh, I am sorry. Bounce back and grow to the light." He said that plants have feelings that are even more sensitive than ours. He could hear them cry when we pulled off a leaf. Although I could not hear them cry, I began to feel some emotion and even some natural movement in the plants when he sat and talked to them. He would say, "A true Cherokee knows how to communicate with the plants. They defended the humans in one of the earliest councils. The plants agreed to be helpers to the humans because they were so young in life's experiences and needed all the help they could get."

In preparing to meditate with a plant, read this section in a comfortable place in the park or somewhere in Nature if it is warm enough for you to go outside.

If not, stay warm indoors then find some indoor plants to communicate with.

Get within arm's reach of a plant or plants to place the plant energy within your energy space. Look intently at the plant. Keep your mind open and relaxed, because you can injure the plant with harsh or angry thoughts. Plants are very sensitive to changing energies in the environment and to the influences around them.

As you focus on the plant look for something you have not noticed about it before. Maybe you will notice the different colors of the flowers or blending of green in the leaves. Without describing these differences or using your critical mind, just smile at the plant. Can you see the increased light around the plant as you smile? The plant will mirror your smile.

Enjoy your new-found friend and feel the comfort of this communication with a plant. The plant will tell you if it is hungry and let you know if it needs a drink. Communication will naturally occur through your own senses as you look at the plant. Practice, keep at it, and enjoy the experience. It will calm your mind and spirit. Maybe you will feel better just by sharing a calming and healing time with a plant.

The first time I tried smiling at a plant, I kept thinking what someone would think if they saw me, and that made me smile even more. The elder said, "Plants have personalities, just like us. Some are stately and proud, while others are gentle and kind. Compliment them on how stately they look or how beautiful their flowers and smiles are."

The Story of the Sun

There are many stories in Cherokee traditions about the Sun. Here is one that always comes to my mind during the summer.

The Sun in the skyway would travel across Mother Earth, giving light for all humans to work in the planting fields. The Sun would smile when she saw the golden corn reflecting the yellow glow of life. Like all of us, the Sun began to feel that the humans did not appreciate what she was doing each day. After all, they never looked up at her or showed any thanks for the warmth and light she provided. Feeling a little irritated, she decided to shine a little brighter as she made her daily journey to visit with her mother, the Moon.

The increased heat and warmth made some of the humans feel more fatigued and dehydrated. Some even became sick as the Sun shone brighter and brighter each day. The people decided to have a council and try to deal with the problem. In council, the fearless Rattlesnake said that he would turn himself into a large animal with horns and scare the Sun. Many in council were concerned that the Sun might be frightened so badly that she would run away and never be seen again. They felt that someone should go visit with the Sun and explain what was happening to the humans on Mother Earth. They wanted her to know that fewer and fewer people were working in the planting fields. They knew they would not be able to survive the long cold winter months without enough food in the storage bins.

Finally they decided to ask one of the elder Medicine Men to go visit with the Sun, explain their plight, and see what would make her happy again. The Medicine Man, named Little Eagle, or "A wo ha li, u s di," started on the long journey to visit the Sun. The Medicine Man turned himself into a huge white bird, to move quickly into the great sky. He knew that he could not get close to the Sun without getting his feathers singed or burned. He was told that the birds today have their bright red colors from getting too close to the Sun. He also knew that the black feathers of birds today became black when their feathers were singed by the Sun on an earlier trip. He carefully planned his trip to come around to the back side of the Sun and gently get her attention with the sound of the Eagle. The Sun liked the gentle and strong call of Little Eagle's voice.

Little Eagle approached the Sun and got her attention by gently calling, "Kaw, kaw, kaw." At first she turned quickly to see Little Eagle and singed its top wings—a mark that still exists on the eagles today. The Medicine Man spent some time talking with the Sun, and she expressed her unhappiness at not being recognized by what she called the "little people" on Mother Earth. Then it was time for Little Eagle to make his long journey back to tell the council what he had learned.

Little Eagle shared his story of what happened when he visited the Sun. He said that since the Sun had a special feeling for the birds, the people could have a special ceremony and dress in feathers to dance, sing, and give thanks to the Sun. They all agreed to have a ceremony to celebrate the Sun and give thanks for the planting and harvesting of corn. They immediately started planning the first Sun Ceremony, with feathers, dancing, songs, drumming, and sharing tobacco with the fire to send a message to the Sun and to the Great One, to honor the Sun and give thanks.

They were so busy that they did not even see Little Eagle disappear. He was nowhere to be found from that day forward. At the beginning of the next planting season a large yellow flower grew at the East side of the planting field. No one could remember anyone planting this flower, nor had they ever seen anything so large and beautiful.

My grandfather told me that some people felt that the Medicine Man, Little Eagle, had gone into the spirit world for a very special purpose. Today, the sunflower is always present in the planting fields and gardens of Cherokees and other Indian people, who continue to give thanks for the Sun.

South: Direction of the Natural

South is the direction of the natural. Cherokee myths speak of the natural existence of life and the boundaries that exist for life to be a balanced ecosystem. In the early years, Cherokee children worked or played in the planting fields and were watched by their parents and older family members while learning about planting and herbs. They learned to respect plants as food. They saw the results of hard work during harvest time. They easily learned respect for Nature and the importance of protecting Mother Earth. The key was innocence, play, and learning respect.

The direction of the South is about following the path of peace to be in harmony with Mother Earth. In ceremonies the color associated with this direction is white or green. The innocence of the direction speaks of the innocence of life. The elders talked of there being many worlds or circles in the Universal Circle of Life. They talked of the interactions between our life and the environment, where there were simple life forms that play and live as we once did in the earliest of times. The elders would say that a star from the Sun would enter the orbits of the planets, just as the Sun was once young as a star and entered our circle. The South represents the innocence of life as a young child.

The Cherokee elders tell this story:

> The Sun and Moon are an equal distance apart now, but they were much closer at one time. The Moon took notice of the Sun and all her warmth and beauty when both were young. Not knowing that Sun was his sister in the Universal Circle, he would come and sit near her to seek her fancy. He would quickly leave when evening came closer and closer. Sun decided to see who he was by carrying out a clever plan. One day when he was near her, she said, "I want to touch your face." He immediately refused and moved away quickly. But before he could move away, Sun threw ashes on his face. That evening when Moon was high and bright in the evening sky, she saw the ashes on his face. Knowing that he was her brother, she never came close to him again. Today, Sun and Moon are equal distances apart from Mother Earth.

In the direction of the South, children learn about the interaction of life and the environment. They learn about the cycles of Nature with water, oxygen, and carbon dioxide, as well as the cycles of life and death. American Indian children on Turtle Island learn that death allows nutrients to be passed into the food chain as soil microorganisms, bacteria, and fungi that regenerate the soil for plants to grow. They understand the life support that these cycles provide for us to survive. As Cherokee we are taught our role as protectors of Mother Earth. It is more a story of regeneration than of evolution. Adaptability has always been the key for survival on Mother Earth. Young children are taught to be adaptable to environmental changes. They are also taught that we as humans have been here a very short time, compared with the animals and plants. We are still very young and innocent in our stage of life in the Universal Circle.

One elder said, "We learn from the animals and the birds. They are our messengers. As Indians we learn to observe Nature and to learn how to survive. They have been here on Mother Earth for many moons. In the scheme of things, we are just a child in the South who is still curious and making mistakes in life. Let's hope the one thing we will learn is to observe the creatures that the Great One has sent here, so we can learn to survive as a tribe."

Maybe, as the Cherokee and the Hopi believe, we are the people of the stars and the Sun. Maybe our destiny is short here on Mother Earth as we learn to adapt to another world. Surely, our future depends on our acceptance of the Old Wisdom in learning to live in harmony and balance, in the way of the Sun and Moon.

5

FRIENDS-MAKING

Early Cherokee ceremonies that had survived by 1920 were the Ripe Corn Ceremony and the Friends-Making Ceremony. As late as 1919, the Friends-Making Ceremony was still being held. It was also called the time of reconciliation or "friends made."

In 1960 I worked with the Cherokee Historical Association in Cherokee, North Carolina. One of my tasks was to search records documenting the early life and ceremonies of the Cherokee. Few written documents were available other than those by Henry Timberlake, James Adair, John Howard Payne, and William Bartram. They recorded their trips into the mountains of North Carolina and what they learned. They could not understand the rationale for certain activities, but when I talked to the elders and asked why things were done a certain way, I learned that some of the information was treated as sacred and therefore was not shared with outsiders. Some Cherokee were willing to share bits of information about the ceremonies to visitors and outsiders. However, none of the Cherokee "informants," as they were called, would violate the old and understood code of ethics, keeping certain things private, for Cherokee people only. I was relieved to see that the only sacrifice on record was the use of tobacco and corn in some form, shared with open fires as a prayer to the Great One. Those prayers were kept sacred and secret, known only to those trained to perform them during certain ceremonies.

The current Fall Festival held each year in Cherokee, North Carolina, during the first week in October, is a combination of the Ripe Corn Ceremony that was held in August with other ceremonies. One elder said, "It [Cherokee Fall Festival] is a time when everyone comes out to see what everybody has been doing during the year. I enjoy looking at all the crafts and food. It's like when everybody canned their own food and you would share with your family and friends. We would go to share our gifts of plenty with others, and they would do the same if they could. We were getting ready for winter. It seems as though winters were much worse back then. Now they go down to the Food Tiger [Lion] and buy what they want each day."

Preparing for Ceremony

Habits are not easy to change, especially when they are learned at an early age. Fortunately for us when we were young Cherokees, the elders would still prepare for winter in the mountains. Their preparations included ceremonies with song and dance, as well as stories of the "old days."

Once I was firing up a gas grill at a community center when an elder came over to me. Like the other elders, he knew I would always listen. The elder started talking about a fifth ceremony, called Friends-Making, which had been lost. The elders often said that the tribe was forgetting many of the old ways and that the young people were no longer interested in the ceremonies. The elder surprised me when he said, "I was a Fire Keeper when I was your age. Now you just turn on a grill and a button lights the fire. We used to start it the old way with dried burdock or whatever we could find while twirling a stick on a wood piece. I have to admit, some of us would use a match. Not me—I was determined. It just took longer. While the others were playing, I would be twirling until I was dizzy. There were seven kinds of wood that we would gather. They were red oak, locus, sycamore, redbud, blackjack oak, hickory, and cedar, or another type of tree to represent your clan. I would stay there until the old Medicine Man from up in Bunches Creek would sprinkle sacred tobacco on the fire and say his prayer. He would put some water with a herb mixture on the fire. Then he would pat me on the head and smile."

Talking Stick

An elder told of the time when he and his friends would carry a stick that had been carved and prepared in a certain way to the Fall Festival. It was symbolic of the time when young men would be chosen to carry the sticks around during the Friends-Making Ceremony. Others would chase after them to be touched by the stick that had been blessed by the Medicine Man. There is an old story about those sticks.

The daughter of the Sun was taken to the darkening land in the West when she was bitten by a snake. Until then, everything had lived forever. The Little People took her in a pine box to have the ghost spirits touch the sycamore sticks to give her spirit back.

While much of the story was considered sacred, we were reminded that the sticks will help bring our spirit back and will help others to regain their spirits. Occasionally I see someone with a stick at Fall Festival. I wonder whether he knows the story and has been chosen to carry a stick prepared and blessed by the Medicine Man.

The Game between the Animals and the Birds

Fall Festival and other early ceremonies were a time for competition and celebration. The story of the game between the animals and the birds has a special place in Cherokee culture: as in early times, the Cherokee enjoy the coming-together time for competition and celebration.

Before there was Indian ball, the animals challenged the birds to have a great ball game. The birds went into council and talked about the challenge. Some of them, such as Chickadee, said that it would be unfair because they were so little. They were reminded that Field Mouse was little, too. Great Hawk said that he was not afraid of any of the animals because he could fly high above them. The birds finally agreed that they were swift and agile, whereas the animals were slow and awkward. They decided to accept the challenge. The Bird Clan leaders met with the Animal Clan leaders to decide on a place to play ball. It was decided that they would go up on a ridge near where the Blue Ridge Parkway is located today in Cherokee, North Carolina. There was a large grassy area, which can still be seen from the parkway.

The animals decided their captain would be the Bear. After all, he was strong, and who could take him down? The birds decided on Eagle for their captain, and Hawk was the co-captain of the bird team.

The animals boasted that they were strong. They even pulled up trees along the way to the playing field to show their strength. This frightened some of the smaller birds. They watched great Terrapin standing still while the animals struck the shell without budging the large turtle. They also watched while Deer demonstrated his enormous speed by outrunning all the other animals. As was the tradition, all the ball players went down to the river, where there was a special ceremony and the animals took a cold plunge. The birds were preening their feathers while waiting. The sacred dance was completed, and it was time for the game to begin.

The animals called for everything small to get out of the way so they would not be stomped into the ground. Two little field mice scurried up the tree to sit by the little birds watching from afar. Eagle saw that they were four-footed, and he asked why they did not go to the animal side of the field. They explained that they had been asked to leave and that the animals had made fun of them because they were so small. Great Eagle said, "Well, you can join us, but we will have to make you some wings." The birds thought and thought about how to make them some wings so they could join in the ball game. Hawk remembered that the drum was still on the ceremonial ground. Knowing that there is always extra skin on the drum, the birds decided to trim a piece of leather for each wing to be tied to the field mice.

The game began, and the ball was thrown up into the air. Of course, Hawk caught the ball. He could have carried it far above the animals on the ground who were looking around at what was happening with awe and surprise. Instead, Hawk threw the ball to one of the field mice with the tied wings. The field mouse caught it in his mouth and glided into the air to the next tree. To this day, he is called Bat. He passed the ball to another mouse with wings, who flew into the air to another tree that was on the animals' side of the playing field. To this day, he is called Flying Squirrel. He threw it to the other birds, who flew and dodged the animals until they scored the points and won the game for the birds. Neither Terrapin nor boastful Bear ever got to even touch the ball.

So it is today that the young Cherokee are taught to never boast about what they can do in competition based on size or strength, but instead to remember the story of the birds and the animals. Young Cherokee learn to always be humble, not to brag, and not to give recognition to themselves, but to recognize the family, clan, and tribe.

West: Direction of Introspection

West is a direction of physical competition, strength, will, and self-awareness. This is the direction for learning introspection, being a helper to others who may be less fortunate physically, and working as a team. Ceremonies have special games such as Indian ball and chunky, a Cherokee game that uses a rock or puck and a stick to move the rock.

It is important to learn confidence as one moves from childhood into adolescence and young adulthood. The values learned are about teamwork and competition to help others, not about winning or showing one's ego as an individual. The stories emphasize that the weaker are supported by the stronger to win the competition. There is a sense of equality because all participants get to play.

The color in the direction of the West is black, a respected color representing the sacred. The darkness of the evening with the Moon energy symbolizes the "darkening land," the direction of the ghost spirits. Early myths told of visits to this land by Little People on behalf of the humans. This could cause some people to overemphasize mysticism in thinking about this direction. However, they should remind themselves that this is the direction of the physical. West reminds us of the thin line between life and death.

Traditional Sacred Truth

In teaching my son, Michael, and my daughter, Melissa, about Cherokee Medicine, I always learned something new about my own truth and I wanted to share with them a few of the truths I had learned. As they were going through young adulthood, I shared with them the story of a young man who decided to find his own way. (I used a woman when talking to my daughter.)

A young man went to a place where the elder Medicine Man would pass each season on his journey in the Four Directions. The young man thought that if he just sat in the center where the paths crossed, the elder would tell him which direction to take. This would make it much easier for him, and it would help him avoid errors and consequences.

On a spring day, the elder came up to the young man. "What are you doing, young man?" he asked. The young man, whose name was Little Deer, told the elder of his plan to get advice from the Medicine Man for his chosen path to follow in life. The Medicine Man thought, then replied, "You must follow your own path." Little Deer said, "Well, you just came from the direction of the North, where it is cold. What did you learn about the North?" The elder told him of his adventure in the North and the lessons to be learned. But he said, "You may have a different experience than I did, so you must find it out for yourself."

Another season went by, and Little Deer continued to sit in the crossroads of life waiting for the Medicine Man to tell him which path to follow. It was summer, the leaves were on the trees, and blooms of flowers and seeds were blowing in the wind. Here came the Medicine Man. The young man asked, "Tell me, sir, what path do you think I should follow?" The elder gave him the same reply as before. Little Deer asked about the elder's experiences in the East. The elder told him of the wonderful gathering of families and clans and their talk of spiritual things. In awe, Little Deer wondered if that might be the direction he should follow. But instead of following that path, Little Deer just sat and waited until the next season. The summer was long and hot, and it seemed that many moons had passed.

Little Deer saw the elder Medicine Man coming toward him as the leaves began to change. Little Deer was changing as well. He was excited to hear what the elder had learned on his adventure in the West, the darkening land. The elder once again reminded Little Deer that it was his choice to follow his own path. He also shared with him the wonderful competitions of games and dances that he had experienced, along with the new dances and songs he had learned. Little Deer was excited, and he thought surely this was the direction for him to follow. But he was a little tired, and he decided to stay for yet another season.

The fall of this life had ceased, and winter was near at hand. Little Deer felt the cold winds and thought that he would freeze to death, with little food and no shelter. Still, he survived another season, waiting for the Medicine Man to come yet again. This time he would really decide which direction would be his path of life. This time the elder did not return to the crossroads, and Little Deer realized that he had now gone through the four seasons of life. Aged and all alone, he realized that he was no longer a young man with a decision to make about his path in life. Life had passed him by while he went through the winter season of his life. He realized that choice was not something to waste because of a fear of consequences, or while waiting for someone else to make one's choice.

Choices are sacred to life's journey. They lie along the path that all of us must follow for ourselves. An important Cherokee lesson is that if you involve yourself in any decision, you also experience the consequences of that decision. It is like knowing the answer to something—but have you received the answer for someone else? Sometimes when guidance has come to you by spirit intervention, it is really a message for someone close to you who is unable to listen to the spirit guide.

Full Circle: Journey of Life

Our choices have consequences, but a lack of choices or a failure to make choices can have consequences as well. When you meditate on giving thanks, it is important to be truly thankful for all the choices you have in life, so you can come full circle with all that life has to offer. Here are some truths about choices to help you, regardless of where you are in your journey or path in life:

- We do have choice. This is gifted to us as humans with a natural will. Choice is a beautiful gift that we often ignore when we are too busy blaming others and lamenting what we do not have.
- Truth is inside of all of us, not just outside of us or somewhere to be found in a foreign country or another place. The Cherokee elders would be the first to say that we have

within us every message and truth that has ever existed. These truths were known by our ancestors, who are always connected to us. We need to listen and understand.

- We can be our own best friend or our own worst enemy. The choice is ours to make. We can keep ourselves "clear" for acceptance of the gifts of life and friends.
- Words are only words unless they express feeling. Expression is a tool for hearing yourself, but listening is a gift for understanding. There is much to be learned in silence and in Nature, which are great teachers.
- The best lessons about good and bad are shown by how we value choices. The true lessons are about being a protector of Mother Earth and a helper to all creation.
- The worst thing about having so many choices is having to choose. The best thing about having choice is the choice to choose.
- The answer is always there before we ask the question. The key is to know how to ask the question to get the real answer.
- Too often we try so hard to be what we are not that we forget who we really are.
- Searching for something is not nearly so hard as knowing what to do with it when we find it.
- The past, present, and future is now. We have everything in our grasp right now, in the present.
- Our imagination is our freedom.
- Humility is our greatest strength.

Truths about choices are based on the Old Wisdom in the Cherokee teachings. An elder said, "If we are looking for our purpose in life, it is easy. Maybe we could save a lot of time by just under-standing this and doing it, rather than wasting time trying to find it out. Our purpose as taught by the Cherokee elders and the Old Wisdom is to be a protector of Mother Earth and a helper to all the creatures that the Great One put here. We are the keeper of all knowledge and all things here on Mother Earth."

The Meaning of the Friends-Making Ceremony

In earlier times, the Friends-Making Ceremony was a way for the families and clans of the tribe to come together. It was a celebra-tion of life and of the survival of the tribe. People shared their clan legends around the sacred fire and told the story of how the plants and animals, along with all creatures, lived in harmony and balance. They were all one family, living in Nature's balance with each other. Then came the human beings. Being young and not understanding the rules of Nature, they started using their gifts to harm the plants and animals. It was necessary for the plants and animals to give of their spirits so the human beings could continue to survive. Therefore, each of us as a human being has a plant or animal spirit that is connected to us.

Human beings had to learn how to live in a harmonious way with their environment. American Indians were the keepers of this Old Wisdom and understanding. This was the only way that hu-man beings could survive. Around the fire at the Friends-Making Ceremony, many stories were told of the beginning, of life, plants as food and medicine, the Sun and Moon, and the old ways. The myths and legends were shared by each keeper of the knowledge. Everyone listened. The story of the clan system was told. The people even dressed in the clan costumes—as the Wolf, Bear, Beaver, Bird, Turtle, Deer, and other clans—to share their story. The most common clan among the Cherokee and possibly the oldest is the Wolf Clan. This is a good clan to discuss in connection with the Friends-Making Ceremony.

The Wolf Clan has probably been around since the beginning of time for the Cherokee, from the time when people would adopt certain animals as their grandparents or guides. They would develop a very close relationship with these animals. The Wolf Clan was called "Ani wah yu" in Cherokee. Names of people were associated with the wolf, such as Two-Wolves, Young Wolf, or just Wolf. The wolves were social animals and kept close to their families, as would the people who were of the Wolf Clan. Few today probably know the story of the beginning of the Wolf Clan. An elder who was a member of the Wolf Clan told it to me, and I have corroborated it from my work with the Cherokee Historical Association.

The people could hear the wolves howling in the night. They were cold and hungry; however, it was well known that eating meat at night was inadvisable because of the wolves. The people lived in wooden homes called longhouses, occupied by many families. The hunters learned about the cunning nature of the wolf and its ability to go quietly through the woods and to move in packs. "The wolves followed a path of harmony, and they did not like anything to upset their way," said the elder. "Wolf was chosen by the Great One to teach the human people how to live in harmony in their families. Wolf was to teach a truth, as each animal would do also for the humans to survive." When I asked about the truth, the elder said, "Wolf teaches us about everything being equal in its own way. Wolf has had many lessons about hunting and living in harmony with its environment."

The elder went on to tell of Wolf's experience in getting caught in the briars, being trapped down a cliff, having birds peck at his head, and getting sharp objects caught in his paws. Wolf teaches patience, even during strong pains of hunger or the desire to satisfy an innate need.

According to legend, Wolf was to be a friend to human beings, and humans were not to hunt wolves. This relationship would result in humans adopting the spirit of Wolf and calling themselves the Wolf Clan. Their symbol would be the head of the wolf, carved on a rock or piece of wood and worn around the neck. When a wolf was found dead, a special ceremony would be held to allow "Wolf Tracker," someone who demonstrated a special gift for tracking wolves, to skin the wolf. The wolf skin would be used only for special hunters, who would wear the skin during a hunting party.

Once a wolf heard the Great One speaking to him. In those days, the humans and the animals spoke one language. Wolf was asked to travel far over the mountains, since the humans were very slow and cumbersome. He would learn a truth that would be shared with the human beings. Wolf started his journey over the rocky edges and in thick woods through Bear country to visit a place near what is now Oak Ridge, Tennessee. Wolf was attacked by a large brown bear when he surprised the bear catching fish in the Little Tennessee River. Wolf was no match for the large bear at short range. He limped away, resting on the river bank, and quickly went into a slumber. Wolf thought he was dead, because he was in the darkening land of the West.

Injured Wolf heard the voice of the Great One saying that he was to continue his journey after the Medicine Man healed his wounds. He awoke but felt very tired and confused. A Medicine Man was wrapping his wounds with plantain leaves tied with fiber. Wolf felt the Medicine Man pack his torn pelt with mud and mixed herbs. He was quickly healed, and the Medicine Man was suddenly gone. During this time Wolf had a vision of human beings sitting around a fire as they celebrated a feast. They sang a song of giving thanks— a song that has long since been lost. Wolf took this truth and lesson back to his friends in the Wolf Clan.

From that day forward a clan feast has included a celebration of giving thanks. All the wolves are invited to partake of the scraps, and the tamed ones stay as long as they want to stay with the human beings. Wolf taught the Wolf Clan people many lessons about survival and how to live in harmony with Nature. They both participated in the Ceremony of Friends-Making.

6

GIVING THANKS

There is a balance and order in the natural environment. The sense of integrity among animals, small creatures, and even plants has much to teach us. To understand it, we must put ourselves into Nature's process of thinking and doing. One of the first lessons we learn is respect for the natural order of things. The entire environment tends to react when something occurs out of order, as when a domesticated cat chases a bird up a tree. The bird respects the tree and understands its vulnerability. The tree provides some protection from the elements. The squirrel lives in the tree, so the bird can be in its space—it already has permission in the natural order of things. A strange-looking cat coming into the protected area does not know to ask for permission to be in the space. The cat upsets the birds, who send a message of fear that upsets the energy in the environment. Other animals start scooting around hurriedly to protect their space. The cat is oblivious to the negative impact it is making because it is focused on the chase and the bird. Nature sustains itself and eventually gets back to some level of natural sanity when the cat misses the bird and finally leaves.

In Nature, everything has its own place and purpose. Humans must work at entering the natural environment in ways that demonstrate cooperative thinking in accordance with the wisdom of Nature. When you meditate on giving thanks, first give thanks for Mother Earth and all the living things: the four-legged ones, the winged ones, and everything that has been touched by the Great One, including even the rocks and trees. Giving thanks is an everyday thing for Native Americans. It shows respect and admits humility. To admit humility is to be open to the gifting of Nature. Not to give thanks, show respect, and admit humility each day is to miss the real beauty of life.

A Cherokee elder said, "To spend so much time on worry and thinking destructive thoughts gives us exactly what we ask for." To spend time giving thanks for whatever we have connects us with our natural self, which is simple and understands simple messages of gladness and giving. In turn, it gives us even more than we can appreciate in life. Each day has a renewed gifting for us.

This meditation will help you reconnect with the sensory side of yourself as you connect with Nature and renew your relationship to all the wonderful sights and sounds around you.

 First, find a place in Nature where you can stay for a couple of hours, perhaps in a park or near a stream under some shady trees. This is the time to learn the power of "Shog wuh," oneness or unity with Nature.

Second, relax and meditate in your own way, or just listen to the sounds of Nature until you feel both your oneness with Nature and "Tile leeh" (two), your likeness to—and difference from—Nature. Feel and sense the connection you have with Nature, and notice where there is a difference. Say to yourself that it is all right to feel the difference, then focus on your oneness with Nature.

Third, focus on going inside to the spirit-self, knowing that the energy of Nature is the circle outside of you. This is "Jawh weeh" (third person), which exists inside you and is able to project outside of your physical and mental inner circle. This takes some practice, but it will eventually come naturally. Sometimes you can focus your relaxed body and fix your mind on Nature's sounds or some other comforting sound such as flute music or drumming. The spirit-self then can emerge with an increased sense of awareness. This sense is very similar to the feeling you have already experienced when communicating with plants.

Fourth, practice the differential by moving in and out of the third person. I call this phasing-in and phasing-out. The expression of four in Cherokee, "Nonk key," is a combination of the physical, mental, spiritual, and natural. Focus on an acute awareness of Nature around you. End this mediation as hunters would end a hunt, with a moment of thanks in the form of prayer and the sharing of tobacco or sage with Mother Earth.

With practice, you can have the feeling of flying with birds or seeing the smallest insect with magnified clarity. It is very similar to a musician's training to listen for differences in sound. The differential is like having a perfect ear for musical pitch. The elder Medicine Men would say that being in touch with all Four Directions at once develops acuity and shifting awareness. In earlier times, hunters would practice to become great hunters. They developed the ability to track animals by using the acute senses beyond smell, hearing, and seeing.

Young Wolf: Get a Life

A Cherokee boy, Young Wolf, was innocent in the ways of life. His father became concerned about his young son because Young Wolf seemed to prefer play and dance over learning the skill of hunting. Young Wolf's father was one of the great hunters among the Cherokee in the Qualla Township. He told Young Wolf that one day he would have to get a life; otherwise life would get him. Puzzled, Young Wolf set out to discover the meaning of his father's words: "Get a life, or life will get you." These words rang in his ears until he knew that he would have to find the answer.

Soon his father planned to be away for several days on a hunting trip. It was near the full moon of the fall, when the leaves were coming down and winter was around the corner. Young Wolf heard of someone called Wise Old Woman who lived in the Cowee District. He heard his mother say that she had special powers and knew about everything. Being only seven, Young Wolf could not make the long trip to Cowee. He appealed to his uncle, who traveled frequently to Cowee to get a sacred stone for carving pipes. He asked his uncle what his father's words meant. The uncle knew he would not be able to explain it in a way that Young Wolf could understand, but he did not want to disappoint the boy. The uncle said, "I think it means for you to do something that would be special in life."

Young Wolf knew that the animals would always be truthful to him. They had been his friends for all his seven years of life. He wondered, though: was dancing the Raccoon Dance not something meaningful in life? It was certainly meaningful to him. He asked his uncle to take some sacred tobacco to Wise Old Woman and ask her that question. The uncle was thinking about seeing her anyway, because he was ready to find a wife, but he needed some sacred tobacco. A deal was struck, and Young Wolf went to get some sacred tobacco from his friend. The friend was the only one to grow the sacred tobacco, and he would not give any to the uncle because he associated with some others who were considered lazy.

Young Wolf went to see his friend Raccoon. They would play chase and he learned much from Raccoon about hiding and climbing trees. "Raccoon, can you tell me how to get a life?" Young Wolf asked Raccoon as they were playing chase. Raccoon seemed puzzled, but responded, "Life is about playing and sneaking food."

Somehow, Young Wolf did not think it was the same for him.

Next he saw Brown Squirrel, and asked him the same question. Brown Squirrel thought for a minute and said, "Oh that is easy. It is hiding acorns and other nuts and seeds so you can find them when it gets cold and snow is on the ground." Again, Young Wolf did not think that this applied to his life, although he hid acorns in the ground as taught by Brown Squirrel, then dug them for his mother when winter hid the ground.

Rabbit was very smart, so Young Wolf thought he might know the answer. Rabbit was hopping through the laurel patch when he heard a familiar voice. "Rabbit, I have a question for you," shouted Young Wolf. Rabbit really liked questions, so he stopped to talk with his friend and listen to his question. Rabbit answered, "Well, for you as a human, it would mean to learn to hunt the animals, but of course, not little defensive rabbits!" They both pondered, then looked at each other and said in unison, "Nope, that is not you."

Once again, Young Wolf continued down the trail looking for the answer to the question before his father returned from the hunting trip.

Young Wolf saw Red Feather, a friend who was about twelve years old, and asked him, "What are you doing?" Red Feather said he was making a strong bow so he could hunt Rabbit. He wanted to please his father by being a hunter. Young Wolf already knew that was not the answer, so he continued his search. Overhead, Eagle was soaring in the sky. Once Eagle had saved Young

Wolf's life when he wandered away from his mother in the planting field. Eagle saw him near a cliff and swooped down to save him from falling off the cliff. Now, Eagle swooped down to see his friend Young Wolf, who was sitting on a stump with a sad face. "What is wrong?" said Eagle. Young Wolf explained his search for an answer to the question. Eagle said the answer was to be responsible, learn to plant food, and be with his family always. Young Wolf thought that was a really good answer, but he still was not sure it was the answer for him.

On his way back toward home, Young Wolf was walking close to the Oconaluftee River. He saw Old Water Dog. Now, Old Water Dog had gone to a conjurer to turn himself into a handsome young Cherokee so he could win the favors of a beautiful young Cherokee girl with long black hair. Maybe Old Water Dog would know something that would help. But Young Wolf knew that the young wife had left as soon as she realized that her spouse was just Old Water Dog. Maybe Young Wolf would not ask him today.

As he continued his trip home he saw Worm Digger, who always worked in the planting fields hoeing and planting. Maybe he would know, so he asked him the question. Worm Digger thought long and hard, then said, "The answer for me would be different than the answer for you. I believe it is for you to find that out for yourself." With that, Young Wolf headed home. He slept that night and waited for the next morning, when his uncle would return from Cowee.

After doing his early morning chores, Young Wolf went to the ceremonial grounds,where he danced around and around. He had learned a new step from Rabbit and from Hawk that he wanted to try for himself. He practiced the Eagle, the Wolf, and the Raccoon Dances. He could hear the drums and rattles with the rustling of the leaves blowing in the wind and with the whispering of the pine trees. The sound of the wind reminded him of the grand ceremonies where all the clans would come together. He saw himself as a dancer, summoned by the Grand Chief at the Grand Council. Suddenly Young Wolf saw his uncle. He knew that he had the answer. The uncle said he had seen Wise Old Woman, who had said that the uncle was not ready for a wife. "What did she say about me getting a life?" The uncle said, "Oh, yeah, well, she said for you to just do well what you do, and you will get your own life." Confused even more, Young Wolf waited for his father to return from the hunting trip.

As the day's sun touched the mountains in the distance, Young Wolf's father came into camp with two large bucks. There was an excitement in the air. His father came and sat down by his son, holding him in his arms. Young Wolf started telling him about his visit with all the animals and the new dance steps he had learned. The drumming started for the ceremony of giving thanks for the gifts of food, and his father fell into a slumber. Young Wolf sang a song he had learned and was sharing the new dance with his father when he saw that his dad was sound asleep. Young Wolf, not wanting to disturb his father, lay in his father's arms and fell asleep himself. Suddenly his father awoke with excitement and said, "Young Wolf, I have had a vision! I saw you dancing some new dance steps like Eagle, Hawk, Wolf, and Raccoon. You were singing a new song as the drumming played a new beat. The Grand Chief summoned you to dance at the Ceremony of Giving Thanks! I was so proud of you! Everyone came to see you, and we feasted with the deer. You were the head dancer." There was silence as Young Wolf hugged his father and smiled, because he now knew how to get a life for himself.

Wolf Medicine

The members of the Cherokee Wolf Clan learned competition, combined with an understanding of the sacred and the traditional. They were great hunters in the early years. They learned much from observing the wolves' behavior, from the early stages of being a young cub to the independence of the lone wolf. Wolves were strong, quick, and fierce in their attack. While not the strongest or the biggest of the animals, they were feared by animals and humans alike. Respect for the wolf and the wolf pack was evident with the Cherokee. It is no surprise that young hunters learned from the wolf cubs lessons about how to play fair, hunt fair, share, and protect the pack from outside harm.

The wolf, or "wah yuh" in Cherokee, was a formidable foe and a friend of the early Cherokee. One of the elders told me that the wolf was a messenger from the spirit world who would help us in new journeys and show us a way to get in touch with the inner self. He also said that many people felt a sense of connection to the wolf as a true brother and spirit keeper. The lesson of the wolf was one of protecting the family or pack, while sharing the meal with others who were deserving. Of course, those not deserving would be banished from the pack. Discipline was key to survival of the wolves, and their strength was in numbers.

The Rabbit and the Wolves

The Cherokee tell a story of Rabbit, who was always bouncing around in the woods and mountains of western North Carolina. The Stomp Dance is still done by the Cherokee today in ceremonies.

> Once Rabbit found himself facing a pack of hungry wolves. Fortunately, Rabbit was cunning, and he knew that his inner fear could make him dinner for the wolves. The wolves' teeth were showing, as with subtle growls they prepared to feast on Rabbit. Rabbit said, "Oh, hello wolf, you are looking fine today!" The first one to speak was Two-Wolves, who was as strong as two wolves and was leader of the pack. He said, "Gee stew [*rabbit* in Cherokee], we are really hungry for rabbit today, and we are thankful that you came along." Rabbit had to think quickly, so he said, "Oh, you don't want to eat me. You would get fur in your teeth. You know how you hate that." The wolves did not seem deterred by Rabbit's plea, and they surrounded him.
>
> Rabbit remembered how much the wolves liked to be the center of attention at the animal ceremonial

gatherings. He told them he knew a new dance they could learn, especially with the gathering just a few moons away. Two-Wolves sat back on his haunches and listened while one of the other wolves pleaded to eat Rabbit for dinner. Rabbit started stomping his big paw to show the wolves the new dance. Actually, Rabbit had just made it up, hoping to get out of this predicament. The wolves started to dance by stomping their paws. Rabbit told them to stomp hard and turn around as they did the Wolf [Stomp] Dance. The wolves were so proud of having a dance named after them that they stomped even harder. While they were absorbed in dancing, Rabbit jumped as high and as far away from the wolves as he could. Knowing that he could not outrun them, he hid in an old stump. When the wolves came to their senses and realized that Rabbit was gone, they went on their way, doing the Stomp Dance.

North: Direction of Sharing

The direction of North is a path of quiet, where the wind can bring messages and where the cold is a friend to those who learn to survive. The North gives us a time of learning and sharing as we become adults in life. We learn generosity in this direction. The wolf and the deer are usually the animals of this direction. The wolf we have just described; the deer is gentle and kind. The lesson of the North is to learn to be kind and gentle in Nature to receive the generosity that Mother Earth and all of Nature have to offer.

The deer is considered sacred by the Cherokee. Its skin is used to wrap sacred objects, such as the crystal that is kept for seeing ahead and for protecting us from other energies and influences. The deer was a favorite meal of the Cherokee. Deer hunters knew how to properly offer prayers and make preparations before hunting the deer. Sacred ceremonies followed the killing of a deer, in which the hunters gave thanks and asked for "clearing," or forgiveness. If this was not done, the hunter would have rheumatism for the rest of his life—or so I was told by the elders.

The color of the North is purple or blue. These colors can be used in candles to "clear" the surrounding area or one's home with a simple prayer of thanks to the Great One for all that we have. I feel honored to be able to share this knowledge and understanding with you. This is the lesson of the direction of the North. This is the meaning of giving thanks.

7

THE SEVENTH-YEAR CEREMONY

The Seventh-Year Cherokee Ceremony has a unique meditation. Whereas many of the old traditional ceremonies used dance, drumming, and song-chants, the "Uku" Dance was done by the chief and high priest. The Cherokee elders whom I learned from could remember little about the ceremonial dance. They did remember the seven "chosen ones" appointed by the priest for certain tasks such as preparing the food and the dance area for ceremony. One important task was the cleansing of the chief with water heated by one of the honored and appointed members. There was a head singer and a head dancer, as used in powwows and traditional gatherings today. The elders also remembered how clean everything was in this sacred place for the Seventh-Year Ceremony. While the chief or priest would normally wear white, everything worn by the chief for this ceremony was dyed yellow. He was not allowed to touch the ground, so a team was appointed to carry him to the center throne in the ceremonial grounds.

When it was time for the chief to perform the Uku Dance, he would move around the circle within the square ceremonial grounds and would nod to those present. They would nod in return. His movements and dance would be imitated around the ceremonial dance area. This would be repeated for three days, and the dance was completed on the fourth day to conclude the ceremony and rituals. As described by the elders, this was a very sacred and honored activity. The meditation for the seven-year Uku Dance was to touch the ground in a sacred way, to understand that Mother Earth is sacred. Every step upon her was and is a dance of life. We draw from her energy, and we honor her with ceremony. As one elder said, "The Seventh-Year Ceremony should really be every seven months to remind us of the importance of clearing our mind and spirit while we reconnect our energy with Mother Earth. After all, we are the same energy, and we need clearing for harmony and healing. To touch Mother Earth is to heal the mind, body, and spirit."

Respect Mother Earth by doing the following mediation:

First, find a place on Mother Earth where you can dance the Uku Dance. I suggest that you do this where there is some privacy, so as to avoid feeling self-conscious or attracting attention. Dance or move slowly in a circle as though you are feeling the earth beneath your feet for the first time. It is all right to wear moccasins or to go barefoot. Imagine moving quietly through the woods as you move and nod to the trees and animals you see. Focus on feeling the movement and showing respect to all things.

Take the time to describe the feeling you had in dancing the Uku Dance, what came to your mind, and how the movements generated different thoughts. Write this experience in a log or notebook to review after a few days. It is a wonderful way to feel the sense of connection with Mother Earth and the stimulation of energy that seems to come from the earth itself. Unlike the other ceremonies, such as the First New Moon of Spring, Green Corn, or even Friends-Making, in this one dance you are alone with your own movements and with the moving energy of Mother Earth. If the idea of a dance bothers you, you can try the same thing while working in your garden by moving your hands on Mother Earth to feel the exchange of energy with Earth itself.

As an elder said to me, "It [Uku Dance] is a way to reconnect to our Earth Mother. Her touch is so gentle, yet so reassuring with each step. As we anticipate the next step we feel the sense of comfort and connection with an energy that we truly understand at some higher level. We are alive, and so is our Earth Mother."

This is a place in the book where I want to express thankfulness for being able to learn many sacred things as part of my Indian Medicine training. The traditonal sacredness of seven cannot be overemphasized. The early Cherokee expression of "Yo wa" represented one universal being. The word itself would not be said aloud by anyone except those trained as traditional priests. Its origin was in the Elder Fires, which came from the sky vault that was involved in the creation of the Universal Circle.

There were seven levels in the sky vault where the Elder Fires were located that created the Sun and the Moon, while creating the forms that we know as Mother Earth and the universe. The creation of the stars and all living things was done by the Sun and the Moon. While all was created by the Great One, "Yo wa," the Elder Fires were there to protect the human beings through the Sun and Moon. After all, they look over us during the day and the night.

In giving thanks in a traditional way, we offer tobacco to the fire, so the smoke becomes a messenger to the Great One and the Elder Fires in the sky vault above. Prayers are offered in the four directions of East, South, West, and North in a counterclockwise direction, then to the lower world or Mother Earth, and to the upper world for the Sacred Seven.

While six ceremonies were celebrated each year by the early Cherokee, the Seventh Ceremony was considered very sacred. Even today, most Cherokees feel a sense of respect and honor when referring to anything with the number seven. The Seventh Ceremony may not be celebrated today among the Eastern Band of Cherokee Indians in North Carolina, but the memory is innately present in song, drumming, dance, feast, competition, and ceremonies of the Fall Festival held each year during the first week of October.

The Sacred Seven

The Sacred Seven shows us the Full Circle Way: we come into this world from the spirit that evolves into a physical form in the womb, and in time we reach the point when we exit this world in physical form to the spirit form again. The concept of seven, or "Gull gwog," reminds us of our own being, which goes through a life process. This process leads us to a sacred spot where we learn our own true reality, "Shog wuh," or oneness with all things in our environment. This is the number one in the Cherokee language and the meaning of unity, or all things coming together.

Our differences from all other things in our environment make us unique. It is obvious that we do not have wings, so we cannot fly. Our ability to think and reason allows us to dream, therefore, we build a way to fly by using an aerodynamic device. However, we know that we can fly in spirit and project ourselves out of our own bodies. There is a physical process in this reality for building an airplane, and there is a mental process for projection. Words presented here in English give you the information, but your own experiences and mental pictures will create the image for you. By seeing the differences, we can make a difference. Ignorance tends to hide truths from us. The Sacred Seven allows us to become a part of the circle or group for interaction and counteraction. By experiencing the circle, we are guided to understand and to balance ourselves with the natural flow of the group, assuming that the group is in balance and is not focused on an "out of phase" place or existence. One elder put it this way: "Sacred Seven teaches us that when we focus on the seven, we are inside of the harmony circle. Of course, like the dream catcher, stuff can get caught in the web of the circle and interfere with good Medicine. You have learned these things so you can be a helper and teacher to others about these lessons." The elder was referring to an understanding that we are in balance with the Sacred Seven when we are in balance with the Four Directions, the lower world, the upper world, and the center of the elder fires. The lesson was about the process for coming full circle, and being in harmony and balance.

Certain assumptions are made about coming full circle and the process of life. First, we understand and accept the differences and the dimensions of being a part of family, clan, and tribe. Another way of putting this is to say that we accept our role in life, whatever it may be. Second, we are independent in our realization that we are who we are, not trying to be someone else or expecting to be accepted as anyone other than who we are. Third, we have mastered something in this life with the gifts given to us. In other words, we have not just squandered our life away making excuses for who we are or what we are not. Fourth, we are generous with our gifts in being a helper to others. This is called "Na wah te" in Cherokee, the balance of energy flow in life. The closest equivalent to this teaching is to be involved with some group process. It may be a formal group therapy approach, a men's drumming group, or a functional family group that allows for open interactions. The Sacred Seven in early Cherokee ceremonies was a way for the family, clan, and tribe to come together for rebalancing and preparation for the next phase of the life cycle.

The ceremonies held by the early Cherokee constituted a group process that renewed values and clarified certain principles of survival and gifting within the group. Maybe if we had six ceremonies to accomplish this today, so many of us would not be in formal therapy sessions. What do we do to get to the next level of the Sacred Seven, or the Seventh Ceremony? We need to realize these important lessons of the Sacred Seven as follows:

- Recognize that people experience difficulties because of the level of disharmony among the Four Directions of physical, mental, spiritual, and natural.

- Recognize that people are what and where they are because of their own decisions, whether independently or because of some influence.
- Animal power teaches us that we can change our situation, our environment, and our life. We have the power of choice.
- We are not alone, and there is a power greater than ourselves that can help us with our choices. We do have the ability to recognize, understand, and move into a place of harmony and balance, regardless of the situation or reality as we may perceive it.
- To use our intent for change, we must first reach out and have someone touch us. That is where our sacred role as a helper comes into play, and our ability to protect through being a part of the Universal Circle, or of a group or family of friends and helpers.
- The process is one of transformation, renewal, or beginning-again as taught in tribal and traditional sacred teachings. This is also the same way of the traditional religious teachings. Many people are searching for "the way." Ironically, the way is right in front of those who accept the teachings without expectations.
- Last but not least, part of the Sacred Seven process is the sweat lodge or the vision quest, which is commonly used in traditional tribal and American Indian and Alaska Native ways. In the next chapter I will take you through this process. Realize, of course, that doing this with words is not the same as going through the actual physical, mental, spiritual, and natural process.

The traditional ceremony of the sweat lodge is the basis of Full Circle teachings, which are open by invitation to those interested. My son, Michael, and I, hold these sessions twice a year on the Cherokee Indian Reservation in North Carolina. While the actual "sweat" is not used, the process takes place in the teachings, drumming, song-chants, activities, and exercises of this group participatory process. There are no rules except that aggression, alcohol, and drugs are not allowed, and egos are left someplace else. Everything is done in the circle and in groups, using the teachings of the Four Directions and the Universal Circle. Each Full Circle has a focused teaching, such as Turtle Medicine, Wolf Medicine, Eagle or Hawk Medicine, which focus on the teachings of a particular ceremony. The basis of the Sweat Lodge Ceremony is always included. More explanation can be found in our book *Medicine of the Cherokee: The Way of Right Relationship.*

The first phase is to enter the circle to come together. As with any group setting, there is a time to warm up to what Full Circle is all about. There is verbal and nonverbal communication; we practice listening to what is not said. The drumming sets the stage for a clearing of the sacred circle and smudging to clear the mind and spirit as we enter the circle gathering. There is a time for "Ou lung sa ta," or crystal vision of having the light shine through.

In the second phase, we see things and see through things by using stories and teachings, much of it interactive. We become able to realize our imbalance by using "crossover" and other techniques that are very traditional and are related to the Old Wisdom. We also better understand the natural consequences of our choices and receive messages from others in the physical world, and possibly from the spirit world or from our own intuition. It is possible that someone may hold onto what has been comfortable.

Each person decides on an individual "crossover" experience using ceremony, water, and traditional techniques in the process.

The third phase is one of purification where we choose and decide to accept and to allow other information or experiences to move on, just as water continues to flow even if we stick our hands into it. For many, this is a time for healing and for new or renewed choices as we choose to experience our own feelings and receive messages.

The fourth phase is an emergence, wherein we reflect, react, and make some decision about restoring harmony and balance in our lives. At this point, the circle becomes supportive. This is called Full Circle, based on the old and traditional teachings of the Sweat Lodge Ceremony and the Cherokee ceremonies of Sacred Seven.

America's Beginning: Sacred Seven

The early Cherokee had an advanced social and political order that was a part of the formation of a constitutional government back in 1827. The Cherokee society established very rational rules on religion, society, and politics. These rules were based on our culture and provided order and organization. The myths and legends told of spirit connections, of guides and guardian spirits. There was one supreme being. There were rituals that showed respect and honor to the elders and to those beloved for their gifts and for being helpers. Saying "thank you" was an integral part of the culture that demonstrated humility and respect to all others.

Witches are found in the Cherokee myths and beliefs, demonstrating the duality of the belief system, much as in other religions of the world. The early Cherokee did not agree with witchcraft, and they even had songs and formulas to dispel acts or fears of witchcraft. Their understanding of the supernatural was very advanced among the Medicine Men and priests of that time.

While there was not a concept of good and bad, there were people who made choices that harmed others in the tribe. Those who harmed others were handled by "dangerous people," conjurors who took care of "bad Medicine." They could be any one in the tribe who had the "gift" of sorcery or witchcraft (which did not in itself make them a bad person). These so-called "dangerous people" dispensed justice outside of the tribal system of law as we know it today. Being confronted by the "dangerous people" was not a fate that anyone would want then or today. "Indian law" grew out of this extremely disciplined way of life. Indian law could result in death, the loss of all possessions, or banishment, which would mean sure death for most at that time.

Medicine Men and Women in early Cherokee history were able to deal with the few diseases of the time. A deadly disease came to Turtle Island with the greedy men of another culture. The disease was smallpox, which became an epidemic. No one of that time knew how to cure this deadly scourge or protect people from it. This was more than Cherokee Medicine or even the conjurors could control. The Cherokee culture and its people welcomed outsiders with open arms, willing to help them survive by teaching them about the herbal remedies and how to grow food. They also accepted Christianity and other religious doctrines, which did not replace the Cherokee way of life. What did bother the Cherokee were lies, greed, abuse, and disrespect for their elders and their families. The Cherokee accepted death as a part of life, but their decisions regarding this event with the Great One was not subject to another culture's court or law.

The Cherokee law was a prevailing moral and sacred order that came from a higher calling and decision. Relationships broke down in those years because of disrespect for the values and order of the Cherokee.

As a Cherokee elder and minister put it, "The social order of the Cherokee society began at one's birth into the seven clans. These clans dealt with rights and obligations. The tribe dealt with ceremony and the sacredness of all things. The deterrents and consequences were handled at a family level within the clans. The values were taught in the stories and teachings of the Old Wisdom, handed down and guided by our ancestors. Every Cherokee knew what it would take to make it through the seven heavens into the sky vault. The seven clans maintained the religion and ceremonies to honor the Great One and to guide the planting and the hunting. Cherokee life was good. The tribe was strong in protecting the rights and relationships of our people. Everyone was equal in relationship and in respect for each other." Tears came to his eyes as he softly spoke.

The elder continued, "At one time, Cherokee had over sixty villages and ceremonial centers, with all the seven hundred people living in harmony. There were beloved men and women, and a council of elders. We had chiefs and priests and 'respected ones' at that time. We had great hunters and ball players. Even the women, who were treated equally, had their own council of women. They made decisions with great influence in the affairs of that time. War was relegated to 'little wars' because no tribe of people could afford to lose their great hunters or their young people. Councils dealt with the problems of political affairs. Our wealth could be measured in the fact that no one went hungry or was cold in the winter. We traded goods with many tribes. Most of all, we loved and cared for each other." The elder paused, then said, "How could anyone or any other culture take that away from a humble people who helped them to survive? They destroyed a nation, but they did not destroy the people. We are still here, proud and humble, even today as Cherokees."

In your meditations, consider an old sacred prayer that was spoken and sung in a prayer chant as the Sacred Seven Prayer in the Seventh-Year Ceremony.

"Ho yan ah, O Great One. Hear the prayer of one who is of the Kee do wa Clan. I have purified my spirit. My feet are on the dust of Mother Earth. I dwell here until I go above the treetops to be with you, O Great One. My way is clear, and not of this earth, as I look straight ahead to my journey. I will be a protector of Mother Earth and a helper to all of your creatures. Ours are the Seven Clans of the Red Clay. We are thankful for your power and love. We seek your guidance, O Great One. We seek the guidance of our ancestors. Our devotion is with you, O Great One. Wah do (Skee)."

Tsa yo gah

AFTERWORD

TURTLE MEDICINE AND BEGINNING-AGAIN

Is it possible for there to really be a beginning-again? The early Cherokee lived a way of life based on beginning-again each year. Renewal was a way of life for a people who had survived many winters, summers, disasters, changes, and diseases. As one elder said, "We not only survived, we thrived! Many [tribes] did not survive. The secret was determination and organization based on strong beliefs and traditions. The term *organization* was to establish and maintain a way of life based on strict guidelines with spirit guides. It seems today that more people want to talk about spirit guides. It is more acceptable today to refer to our ancestors as a real spirit connection. They gave us life, and they continue to guide us every day of our lives."

How do we begin-again? Turtle Medicine provides guidance for the beginning-again activities and for a way of life that enables us to clear our past and prepare for our new journey. Someone once said that what I was sharing was New Age. I told them that my teachers called it Old Wisdom. Whatever people want to call it is fine with me—it is really new people learning Old Wisdom. My teachers were very careful when giving things names but were very accepting of how people expressed their own feelings about the traditions they were taught.

I am a student of Nature and science. To understand either, one must observe with a certain amount of trust and respect for what is being observed, and then draw conclusions. I see no difference in how the early Cherokee learned Medicine and how science reaches a result, except for spirit guidance. However, I suspect that all scientists get spirit guidance, along with their gut feelings about what they are studying. Our Cherokee ancestors were not able to do a literature search, so talking with others about study and spirit guidance helped them reduce errors in postulating and proposing a starting point. The experience of a young Cherokee man and his interest in a young Cherokee woman, as described by Cherokee elder, may serve as an example.

The young man was observing a young woman as she danced at a ceremonial gathering. The elder asked him what he observed about the young woman. He described her long dark hair, flowing in the breeze, which attracted his attention. He also mentioned that she had a certain look and smile, but he figured that she would probably not be interested in him. The elder told the young man to observe many young women for the next seven moons, but to be sure to pay some attention to those who mirrored his glance and returned his smile. He also told him to become friends with these young women, but to keep some distance, so he could maintain a clear perspective. Last, he told him to observe how the young women who responded to him were also responding to other young Cherokee men. The experiment was based only on the limited number of young women in the age group being observed.

Things were going well for the young Cherokee man, until his objectivity was challenged by one woman, who did not follow the custom of having her older brother speak for her. Maybe she did not have an older brother or someone who would play this traditional role; certainly this factor was not anticipated in the initial setup of the experiment. The young woman came over to the young man and asked him to meet her at the old chestnut tree, a place often used by young men courting young women. This shy and reserved young man met her at the chestnut tree, partly out of fear of being ridiculed if he did not. When they were all alone, she said that she had had her eye on him for some time. He admitted that he did not really have his eye on her, as she was not one of the girls he had been observing. Having expected quite another response, the young woman became very upset. He tried to explain about the instructions he had received from the elder, but she did not hear anything he said. She immediately went back and told the others that he had lured her out to meet with him without permission from her family.

You can imagine how the rest of this story went, with consequences taken and lessons learned. The experiment had to be ended because the subjects—the young women—would not look at the young Cherokee man again. He was shunned by them, as was the Cherokee tradition. As the elder described it, the young man did not follow the Cherokee rule of always following one's spirit guidance for a successful conclusion in a life experiment. (Of course, this could also be a moral about being taken in by foolish pride.)

There was a good ending to this story, according to the elder. What happened to this young man was mentioned in a council of elders, and the young woman was asked to recant her story and to tell the truth. The young man began-again with a proper protocol, so to speak. He finally did establish a proper courting relationship with a young woman, and they joined with the blessings of their families and the elders. The young Cherokee woman also found someone who fancied her, and the couple received the same blessings from families and elders.

With the teachings of Turtle Medicine, can we have a beginning-again as a renewal of our lives? To understand how, we must know something more about Turtle Medicine and about the sacredness of the turtle as held by Native Americans. The turtle is considered to be one of the wisest of all creatures, having been around since the beginning of Mother Earth. The turtle was especially chosen by the Great One to support Mother Earth on its back and is sacred. Mud turtle soup is delicacy today, but to Native Americans the gift of the turtle was a food of honor and special power. The turtle's hard shell was used only in certain ceremonies as a rattle, and it was worn by the women in special dances. To witness or participate in these dances was a special honor. One had to be trained in Turtle Medicine before being chosen to wear these rattles or use the turtle rattle in song-chants.

Unlike the ceremonies such as the Green Corn Ceremony, which provided renewal, Turtle Medicine was about being reborn by going through certain rites to give Mother Earth the baggage we had been carrying around. Only then could one receive the freedom of flight from the trials of this life. After going through this experience, there was only one way to live, which was to be a helper to all others and a protector of Mother Earth. Expressions such as "following the Red Road," or "living a good Medicine way" are common American Indian expressions. This commitment was and still is taken seriously by American Indians. It transcends all other commitments in life. For some tribes it starts with a sweat and a vision quest; for others it is a personal achievement in life that is treated in a very humble way and without pomp and ceremony. It is my intent to describe what we can do, without oversimplifying or disrespecting the sacredness of Turtle Medicine.

Here is a guided activity that I want you to consider trying for a period of seven days, or seven weeks, or seven months. It is easy to follow, and it can help you follow the path of Turtle as you learn the way of Turtle Medicine.

Participate in a Native American circle that is guided by spiritual activities for conducting a vision quest or a sweat lodge, or just being in a circle of traditional teachings for a weekend. Be willing to be open and to allow guidance to come to you. Such activities will open your heart and help you shut off your thinking long enough to allow you to receive messages. If you cannot do that, find some friends who will support you in a circle gathering of like-minded people who help one another find their own spiritual paths. This could be a drumming group, a Native American Circle gathering, or just a few close friends. You might just sit in the middle of a circle of rocks or plants that create a circle of energy.

Meditate on understanding the Lesson of Seven. The old Cherokee teaching of "Ki tu wa" or "Ki do wa" gave its name to one of the original seven mother towns in North Carolina. The town of Kituwah was a center for unique tribal interpretation of beliefs. The oldest priesthood probably existed there. As it was a secret society, only a few were invited to participate. The Lesson of Seven focused on clearing one's self for seven days and nights by fasting, ceremony, and prayer. On the seventh night, the spirit of Thunder Boys or thunder and lightning would bring in a vision as a message from the Universal Spirit.

The Lesson of Seven is a time of structured listening to ourselves and our spirit guides. The lessons come in bits and pieces to form a picture that we are to see for ourselves. Sometimes the Thunder Beings come to us in the form of a shock or "awakening." The message is usually very powerful.

This practice was traditionally done every seven years, starting with the seventh month of the year during the new moon. A Cherokee elder once told me it would be done every year, based on the old Cherokee calendar starting with the first full moon in January, which would make the seventh moon the new moon of August. The seventh year would be the time to seek Turtle Medicine for starting life as a beginning-again time. It would be a time to have a special ceremony with a fire outside, using a circle of rocks to protect the spirit of a person inside the circle. The person would start with a sweat on the first night and go into a sweat on the seventh night, staying awake all night on the seventh night to greet the rising sun and the new beginning-again.

To practice the Lesson of Seven, make sure you have consistency in the structure of time and place that is protected and allows you quiet. Find a quiet time without interruption on each of seven nights. Light a purple or blue candle in a dark space or room, and meditate in any position that is comfortable.

Protect yourself with strong images of light or the spirits of ancestors who are there to protect you from unwanted spirits or influences. Always make it very clear that only those spirits that you allow to be with you may be present. All others are to stay away from your protected space. This is your sacred space, which allows you to be totally open and relaxed to receive the spirit gifts. I do not recommend being in your bed; rather, take a comfortable position on the floor or on the ground. This is a special time and a special place for a new or renewed experience. Use a song or a drum to usher in spirit guidance. When you stop the song or drum, listen in silence for the messages or images that put together a picture.

Always give thanks to the Great One and to all things that provide you with life. Even your difficult memories and experiences can become a way for you to begin-again and be a better helper to others.

Talk to some trustworthy friends about your experiences in meditation. They can help you clarify your experiences and messages. Remember that messages can come in the form of words or pictures. You may picture yourself, or you may be represented by someone else or something else in the picture. Just enjoy the experience, and allow more than the serious side of yourself to participate.

An old story tells of the tenacity of Turtle in traveling to meet the sun. While slow, Turtle never sways from its path and will continue over many obstacles to reach its destination. While many of the Turtle stories in the Cherokee heritage were lost, here is one that was told to me by a Natchez-Cherokee elder.

> Most of you have heard the story of the race between the Rabbit and the Terrapin, but few have heard the story of Turtle not being chosen to be among the select few to travel for a council with the Sun and her daughter. There was a time when Sun, Nu dah as she was called, would travel in the early morning across the sky vault to visit Grandmother Moon. Each day she would stop at about noon to rest while she had lunch. Often her daughter would travel with her. Being young, she would have to stop, go to the bathroom, and play. The Little People would be working in the planting fields to get the corn, beans, and squash ready for harvest and the Fall Green Corn Ceremony. But the Little People were getting sick and could not work in the long, hot noonday light. They decided to meet in council to see who would travel for a meeting with Sun to solve the problem.
>
> As some of you have heard, two of the Little People agreed to make Medicine and change themselves into snakes—Rattlesnake and Copperhead. They planned to sit by the door until Sun came out for her travels, then bite her. They tried this, but of course Rattlesnake made so much noise that it alerted Sun. She chopped off Rattlesnake's head and blinded Copperhead, so all he could do was just keep biting without getting close to her. She said, "Get away, you nasty snakes," and began her travel to visit Grandmother Moon. It seems

as though the Snake tribe has never had much luck in affairs of council. Another of the Little People decided to turn himself into a giant snake, or Uk te na, with large horns to scare Sun. Of course he was not successful, and he returned having forgotten what he was there to do. Some may have heard that Rattlesnake bit the daughter, but that is another story about our mortality here on Mother Earth.

What I want you to hear right now is that because the Snake tribe made such a mess of this whole situation, a Medicine Man came forward to be a helper to the Little People. Instead of solving the problem, Sun grieved the passing of her daughter, and she would not come out of her resting place in the sky vault. For many moons the sky was dark, and the planting fields did not produce.

Turtle had listened to what was happening in council. Of course, no one would listen to him. He approached the Medicine Man and told of what had happened. Plants and life on Mother Earth depended on Sun making her trip each day. Turtle was willing to gift himself to the Medicine Man to make a sacred turtle rattle. This would be used for a special song-chant to lull Sun out of her resting place. This was done while the Little People took Sun's daughter in a pine box to the Darkening Land for the spirits to return life to her.

So it was that the Medicine Man agreed to turn himself into a large white eagle and fly quickly to the place of the sun. With his special turtle rattle containing dried corn nuggets, he chanted a special song-chant: "Hey ya, ah hey eh hey yah, Nu dah, Nu dah, Nu dah, Nu dah, ho, ho, ho, e, hi ya yo, hi ya yo, Nu dah. Ah Ho!" It was a song of friendship, asking Sun to listen and understand how much we needed her. She slowly came out of her resting place.

You know the rest of the story. The Medicine Man never returned, but each planting season at least seven sunflowers appear on the east side of the planting field. And of course, Sun continues her travel each day to Grandmother Moon's place.

It is important to understand that Turtle made a bold gesture to be a helper with the ultimate cost to himself. Even today the Medicine Man has a sacred instrument to accompany him while he sings his special song. This is sung at every Friends-Making Ceremony and Sun Ceremony. It is a reminder of how the Little People were so important to the Cherokee at an earlier time. To this day, the turtle rattle is used only for special Medicine and at special ceremonies that celebrate times of renewal.

Today is a time of Turtle Medicine. All of us are ready for a beginning-again in our lives! This is a time of peace, or "Toe he," in our renewed lives. It is a time for sunshine, or "A ga lee ha," to come through within our spirits as if we were small children seeing something new and thrilling for the first time. It is a time of healing, or *"Do he ye."* It is the time for us to realize that the word *human* comes from the rich humus of Mother Earth, while the *being* means that we are to be in harmony and balance with all things in the spirit of Nature. We truly are gifted as a helper to all other living things and as a protector of Mother Earth.

Doc Amoneeta Sequoyah said, "We are more than life. We are the connection to our ancestors. We are the bridge to the future of our children, who will be us in another time, and the circle of life goes on just as it has for many millions of moons since the beginning of time. Each day is a new beginning. Each evening is a new beginning-again. Ho Yan Nah!" He would chant his favorite song-chant, giving thanks to the Great One for the gift of life. At his last breath, he was chanting. "Oh he ho e, oh gi daw da, he ya yo, he ya yo, ha da nan ste ga i, a ni e Law hi, Ah ho yah, Ah ho yah, a ho yah, Ah ho yah, HOH!" Someone who overheard him speaking in Cherokee said that he was reaching out for the hand of his father, who would take him across the Smoky Mountains to a place in the setting Sun. The spirit chant could be heard in an adjoining room. As he often said, he was the last of his kind. He also said that there was a new day dawning when the young and elder Medicine Men and Women would come into their own with a renewal of the Old Wisdom. The old Cherokee crystal would be found again, and people would understood that the Cherokee were truly a sacred people. In his last moments, he saw Turtle cross his path as life was beginning-again.

Touch the Moment

Several times in my life I have felt close to the point of passing on to the other world. Probably the first time, though I was too young to remember it, I fell off of the bed while a neighbor was watching me. I do remember something that occurred when I was about twelve years old. I was very sick with the flu—so sick that I kept losing consciousness. That was my first experience of being in the spirit world. I could hear voices and see spirit people as though there was a whole world beyond what conscious reality.

I met a little girl dressed in deerskin, who was carrying a flower. Somehow, I knew that she was called Little Flower. At first I was afraid, because I really had no concept of death. In retrospect, I must have been having a near-death experience, although I was told that I was just hallucinating due to having a high fever. For me the experience was about another reality. It was the beginning of my spirit friendship with Little Flower.

Little Flower would come to me in various ways to get my attention. Of course, I would never tell anybody, not even my closest friends. My special friend would cause my nose to itch, or a grasshopper would hop up into my hand. Once while playing baseball I was on third base. A butterfly kept flying around my face. I knew it was Little Flower playing a trick on me, as though I was a flower attracting the butterfly. A fly ball came my way, and it hit me right on the head. Boy, was I embarrassed. A friend told me to start watching the game and quit playing with a butterfly. That one time, I slipped and said that it was Little Flower sending the butterfly to trick me. He just looked at me strangely and walked back to second base.

These Little People, or spirit friends come to us to give a special message or to protect us in some way. While attending Western Carolina College I had another near-death experience. I lost all control of my body while in class, and I was taken to the infirmary, totally unconscious for several minutes. My pulse had stopped. As I found myself moving into another reality, there was Little Flower to meet me. She seemed older, as though she was aging while I was aging, instead of being caught in time and space. That seemed very strange to me. While I cannot remember anything that went on while I was in this other reality, I do remember a feeling of calm and the presence of a bright or healing energy. My last memory was of something that Little Flower told me to remember: "Touch the moment."

The following years found many of us going from college to war during the Vietnam conflict. I always remembered to touch the moment, as though no other moment existed or as though this moment would never come again. It is an awareness or presence that keeps us in contact with this reality. Truly, what was will never be again. We are given a gift of a particular moment that is either wasted or fully appreciated. This carried me through a war, a difficult career, and the challenges of life from that moment on through today. Even at other critical times in my life, I felt complete and calm because I knew that I was experiencing life in a positive and spiritual way. Challenges such as the passing of my father and my sister were moments when I felt a very special connection with both persons I loved in this reality, knowing I could communicate with them in the other reality. I also learned that I have received an important lesson in Indian Medicine and experienced it for myself.

I believe that many people have similar experiences involving the spirit world that they do not discuss, primarily because they fear criticism or public opinion. However, I do believe that we are more open today because of books, television programs, and movies that are presenting this phenomenon in a positive way. There was a time when I would not speak of my experience with Indian Medicine. Now I believe that more people are curious about this very old traditional way of teaching and life. It is important to understand that it is a way of life. I can still lead my career as a health professional, yet follow the way of life and traditional teachings of Indian Medicine. They include the physical, mental, spiritual, and natural aspects of life in the environment that makes up our circle or Universal Circle. Belief in the spirit world as a reality that we share is a part of that way of life. Little Flower is part of the spirit world that is connected to me. Understanding this connection means that we are more connected than we may ever really accept at this time. However, I was told by one Cherokee elder that in the near future we would be more accepting of spirit people. He also said that in a vision he saw that more of them would be among us as of 2001.

I asked one of the Cherokee elders how we could "touch the moment." She looked surprised and responded, "To hear this message is to know the spirit world with personal experience. Few really understand the importance of being able to experience a moment in time and accepting whatever is happening as a special moment. It could be looking into someone's eyes, or watching the birth of a baby, or experiencing something in Nature that helps you realize the fragility and beauty of life. It is more than a moment in time; it is a memory that connects us to all time."

Coming Full Circle

We have come full circle in our journey through Cherokee meditations. We started in the beginning, went through the ceremonies of life, and we learned the value of the Sacred Seven. As all things end in Cherokee traditional teachings, there is no goodbye in the Cherokee language. We can only come full circle and begin-again. I encourage all readers to learn to touch the moment and to know their value as protectors of Mother Earth and helpers to all creations in the Circle of Life. A Cherokee elder said, "As the Sun sets, so does the Moon rise in the sky. While one gives us light and survival of life, the other gives us survival through darkness as we rest to meet the beginning again. This is the way of all creations in the Universal Circle. We must always remember to give thanks each day in a meditative way. It is the way to clear our minds, to heal our bodies, and to mend our hearts as we come full circle again to begin-again."

There is so much that we do not understand about the spirit connections and beginning-again. A Natchez-Cherokee elder once said, "Everything that is, always was and will always be again. There is nothing new, only new again. Even the greatest of all technology is not greater than anything that was great before this century or this time. Yet, what is greater than the simplicity and complexity of life itself."

In your final meditation, prepare yourself as usual by sitting quietly in your special place. Imagine your own spirit connection with all the experiences you have had in your life. Maybe that road sign you keep seeing is a message or sign about something specific in your life. Maybe that dream or vision has a special connection with someone else you know or whom you will meet in this life. Whatever your connections may be in this life and with the spirit world, there is a Cherokee or other tribal or religious teaching to explain those connections and your role as a helper and protector of all the other beings and of Mother Earth.

O Great One,

Thank you for the Spirit of the Wind,

> *It stirs my spirit and sends messages to my heart.*

I thank you for the spirit of Mother Earth,

> *As I listen to the drum beat,*

>> *I hear the heart beat that gives us life.*

O Great One,

I thank you for the Ancestors and the teachings,

> *That guide our way of life here on Mother Earth.*

I will forever hold sacred the pipe of peace,

> *And I will share the tobacco for prayer,*

>> *As I give thanks to the elders and the Ancient Fire.*

O Great One,

I give thanks in the way of the Red Clay people,

> *Oh gi daw da, ga lun la di ehi, Wa do (Skee).*

Sa Yo Gah